Literature as Testimony 1

The Austrian Anschluss
in History and Literature

ARLEN ACADEMIC

The Austrian Anschluss in History and Literature
Eoin Bourke

James Liddy: A Critical Study
Brian Arkins

Conserving the Emerald Tiger
George Taylor

Exploring John's Gospel: Reading, Interpretation and Knowledge
Colm Luibheid

Nineteenth-Century Ireland Through German Eyes
Eoin Bourke

The Austrian Anschluss
in History and Literature

Eoin Bourke

Arlen House
Galway
2000

First published in December 2000

Published by Arlen House
PO Box 222
Galway
Ireland

and

42 Grange Abbey Road
Baldoyle
Dublin 13

L198.354
€30.00
830.914

ISBN paperback 1–903631–05–X
ISBN hardback 1–903631–06–1

www.arlenhouse.ie

Cover design by Dunleavy Design, Salthill, Galway
Typesetting: Arlen House
Printed by: ColourBooks, Baldoyle Industrial Estate, Dublin 13.

for Stella Rotenberg

Acknowledgements

I wish to thank my friend, the Austrian poet and prose-writer Richard Wall, and my colleagues Dr. Róisín Healy and Ursula Huemer of NUI, Galway for some invaluable pointers, Mary Lyons and Eva Bourke for their voluntary and painstaking proofreading, as well as the Royal Irish Academy and the *Österreichische Akademie der Wissenschaften* for making possible a research sojourn in Vienna in the summer of 1996. I also wish to express my gratitude to Dr. Elisabeth Klamper of the *Dokumentationsarchiv des österreichischen Widerstandes*, Konstantin Kaiser of the *Theodor Kramer Gesellschaft*, Andrea Strutz of the *Abteilung für Zeitgeschichte* at Graz University and Dr. Michael Postl of the Austrian Embassy, Dublin, all of whom helped by readily and promptly supplying information and texts. I also wish to thank the National University of Ireland, and Professor Tom Boylan, Dean of Research at NUI, Galway for their generous publication subsidies as well as the Millenium Committee on Research at NUI, Galway, for a research grant. The reproduction of the photographs on the front and back covers is by kind permission of the *Institut für Zeitgeschichte an der Universität Wien*.

Contents

The concept "Workbook"

The practice of writing commentaries on the margin of book pages is more widespread among German students than here. One's reception of a book of secondary literature in a German university library or from a second-hand bookshop is not infrequently enriched by what some would consider the defacement of the book: added to the perspective represented by the scholarly author(s) on the literary subject being treated and one's own critical reading of that perspective there is often added a third view in the form of a running commentary by some anonymous reader who got to the book before oneself: marginal notes, exclamation marks or differently coloured underscorings. These comments can frequently be insightful, are usually argumentative, sometimes bluntly aggressive ("Quatsch!"), but almost always thought-provoking, although the last kind, the curt rebuttal, is the least satisfying in that it does not give us access to the anonymous disputant's reasoning. These intrusions from elsewhere remind one of the existence of a world extraneous to the triad of self/writer/scholar and throw open new avenues of thought often in opposite directions to one's own, the scholar's or even the author's. To encourage the English-language student or teacher to do the same, we have left an extra-wide outer margin on each page in the hope that they will, as a result of the added space, articulate why they think something is nonsense.

Not that we wish to encourage the defacement of library books, however creative graffiti can sometimes be. But we would like to instrumentalize the idea for readers with their own text-books, invite them to join, enliven and extend the debate initiated by the text by way of their own annotations, insertions, cross-references, contradictions, rectifications and spontaneous – or better still – considered reactions to what is being said and quoted. The word "workbook", therefore, is being used here in a loose sense, to mean a textbook into which notes of one's own can be comfortably and meaningfully added. It is also a public admission to the effect that such a textbook can lay no claim to completeness. In the field of Cultural Studies no assertion can ever be final but rather, by dint of the very discursive nature of the discipline, always must invite modification or expansion. Moreover, literary texts can never meet with their final and definitive interpretation, no matter how erudite and perceptive the interpreter, and in a series such as that planned under the rubric "Literature as Testimony", the constant consulting of historiography in order to contextualize the literary text transports the discourse into an area where claims to infallibility are particularly out of place. In historical accounts there will always be a different selection of facts to that in the text, different perspectives, agendas and focuses. The "Notes" margin, therefore, is inserted with mainly teachers of German literature and history in mind, so that they can shape the material to their own ends by selection, supplementation and discussion. But it is also there to challenge individual readers and students to be more than mere recipients: to bring their own thinking and knowledge to bear, to complement or question in their own handwriting what they read – to become, in a sense, co-authors, if only in pencil. We feel that such a book, if accompanied by many thoughtful marginal notes by the readers, might remain a source of satisfaction to them beyond the usual lifespan of interest generated by a densely printed book by a supposedly omniscient author.

We hope to continue this series of Galway German Workbooks on Literature as Testimony at regular intervals. These are some of the themes which are being considered as future workbooks.

- The Thirty Years' War
- Witches in History and Literature
- *Vormärz* and 1848
- Nineteenth-Century Ireland through German Eyes
- German Colonialism
- German Urbanisation and Berlin
- "Die Stunde Null"
- The Student Revolt of 1968
- "Gastarbeiter": Immigrants, Second and Third Generation
- "Die Wende"

Preface

Literature as Testimony

> *"Das Poetische hat immer recht;*
> *es wächst weit über das*
> *Historische hinaus ..."*
>
> *(Wilibald Schmidt in Theodore*
> *Fontane's "Frau Jenny Treibel")*

My main concern in conceiving of a series under the rubric "Literature as Testimony", as well as in offering this book as its starting point, was a pædagogic one. The series is being launched with an eye not to the academic debate on New Historicism, or for that matter to any other current meta-theoretical debate, but rather more pragmatically to the problems of teaching and imbibing German language, literature, culture and socio-political history in non-German places of learning. Basically: how does one bring across literary texts to a generation of young people who have grown up in an entirely different socialization process and code system from the one they are studying, far away from and long after the "scene of the action" which we as teachers of German Studies are expected to impart? One way, by no means the only one, is to combine historical narrative and literary analysis: to use those literary texts which were documents of witness and critique at nodal points of history or of recollection and critical re-examination in their aftermath, and to allow historical narratives and literary texts to interact. At the same time, one has to take Hans Mayer's admonition to heart: "die Werke der Schriftsteller nicht als Indizien für Historisches zu benutzen, folglich zu mißbrauchen, sondern als Schöpfungen eigenen Rechts zu nehmen."[i] The intention, therefore, is more than to use literary texts purely to enliven the retelling of historical events: rather, it is to show how literary texts also *deepen* that retelling, to demonstrate their seismographic nature, i.e. their ability to spotlight, condense and illuminate historical conditions, epochs and turning points in a more profound way than most other kinds of texts. The historical contextualization, on the other hand, should have the effect that the students learn not only self-contained literary history with a conventional emphasis on aesthetics, questions of form and authorial biography but also important aspects of German/Austrian/Swiss socio-cultural history.

In this volume I have tried to demonstrate how this can be done with reference to the so-called Anschluss. The combination, I hope, will awaken in students and readers a sense of both the bizarreness of those events and the daily terror – to use Hannah Arendt's much quoted phrase, "the banality of evil" – engendered by them, as well as the power of both contemporaneous and retrospective literary texts to re-stage and bring back to life in a succinct, evocative and sometimes provocative manner that contradictory bizarreness and terror which the extremely important but dry accumulation of statistical facts cannot concretize in the same way. As Heinrich Heine put it in *Reise von München nach Genua*, people demand their history out of the hand of the poet rather than of the historian. "Die Geschichte wird nicht von den Dichtern verfälscht. Sie geben den Sinn derselben ganz treu, und sei es auch durch selbsterfundene Gestalten und Umstände."[ii] Like Fontane's character Wilibald Schmidt quoted in the motto above, Heine compares and evaluates the two disciplines and comes down firmly in favour of his own. While I have no intention of prioritizing in this way, I do wish to make felt that literary texts combine the public and the private, the objective and subjective, in a way that historiography does not allow, and as such is an indispensable complement to history-writing. To quote the sadly neglected Austrian novelist Franz Kain:

> Die Geschichts-Wissenschaft zielt auf Aktenschrank und Zeugnistruhe der Historie, die Literatur wühlt lieber in deren ungeordneten Wäscheschränken. Der Historiker hat es auf Überblick und Zusammenhänge abgesehen, die Literatur mehr auf das Detail und die inneren Vorgänge. Der Historiker will die Zeit selbst in ihren bewußt und unbewußt hinterlassenen Testamenten dokumentieren, der Literatur ist es mehr um das Leben in der Zeit zu tun, sie befragt lieber die Hausmeisterin als den Amtsvorstand. Der Historiker deckt Ursachen für allerlei Erscheinungen auf, die Literatur gestaltet Folgen und Wirkungen. Die Geschichtsschreibung setzt die Einzelheiten zu einem Gesamtbild zusammen, die Literatur nimmt es auf sich, darzustellen, wie den Menschen bei diesem oder jenem Knoten der Geschichte zumute gewesen ist.[iii]

To illustrate what Kain has so well expressed above I have cited various literary texts drawn from prose, poetry and drama. In painting in the historical background I have omitted to delve too deeply into the pre-history of the Anschluss (the long history of the Anschluss idea, which had, surprisingly, many advocates on the Left as well as on the Right, albeit for very different reasons, or the so-called *Februarkämpfe* of 1934, which made the 1938 Annexation all the smoother by the fact that Dollfuß had already crushed the anti-fascist organizations of the Left). Every pre-history has in turn its own pre-histories – some commentators even see the origins of the Third Reich in the Thirty Years' War – and every attempt to paint the whole picture from beginning to end would take us back too far.

I have also tried to avoid absorbing the reader too much in the purely political and military history, that is, the events that took place in the so-called corridors of power. This story has been told grippingly in Hellmut Andics's *Der Staat, den keiner wollte*: the Seyß-Inquart telegram that was never sent, the logistic chaos of the German invasion, the frantic negotiations of the Roman Catholic hierarchy with the Nazis, the reasons why the Social Democrat Karl Renner recommended a vote for Annexation in April 1938. Instead, I wanted to emphasize history as seen by those who feel the brunt of it: how the events dictated from above impinged on the lives of ordinary citizens and people on the margins as conveyed by eye-witness accounts, literary impressions and memoirs.

Not all of the texts are based on personal experiences. Friedrich Torberg, for instance, left Austria before the Anschluss and wrote his account of those days in his novel *Auch das war Wien* while fleeing before fascism from Vienna to Prague and from Prague to Paris. Felix Mitterer was not yet born when the Third Reich came to an ignominious end. But writers do not need to have been personally on the spot to write an authentic literary evocation of what went on in their absence as well as an incisive analysis of the mass psychology of the moment.

Some of the poems quoted are famous and to be found frequently in anthologies, while others are decidedly non-canonical. Among the latter there is the occasional one that would probably not stand up to the kind of intensive æsthetic-evaluative analysis to which pure literary studies are prone, but that is irrelevant: they derive their legitimization from their historical authenticity, and as such will come to life and probably appeal in their unhewn immediacy all the more to students and readers of walks of life closer to those of the poets in question. Whether or not, they and other readers are called upon to register their views on the margin.

The centrepiece of the treatise is an in-depth analysis of Ernst Jandl's extraordinary "wien: heldenplatz", written many years after the event described. Here in particular the readers are invited to pursue any personal linguistic associations that might be set off for them by the text. The scholars quoted, particularly Jörg Drews and Peter Pabisch, ranged far further afield than in this essay in their search for possible clues, whereas I confined my quotations to those interpretative forays of theirs that I personally found plausible. The other poems quoted are more transparent and are explained by the context. Much prosework has been excerpted, a few dramas have been drawn from, and extra-literary texts such as diary entries and letters are also quoted to complete the picture by providing micro-histories. If a certain amount of emphasis was placed on lyrical poetry, that was for a reason: it is probably one of the hardest genres to teach, because in my experience students bring with them from secondary school some very false ideas of what constitutes poetry – transcendence, sublimity, a concern primarily with the "great themes" of love and death – which predispose many students to reject it out of hand as a mode of expression irrelevant to their everyday lives. However, the lyrical texts contained in this essay give far more an impression of urgency and actuality than some students might expect of poetry through the fact that they are artistic responses to specific historical events. Poems also have the advantage that they can be reproduced *in toto* in the framework of such a book. The hope is that, by filling out the historical background, the value, poignancy and functionality of the texts will be better appreciated by an otherwise unresponsive audience.

When excerpting from prose and drama, I attempted to do so in a way that the text particles made sense in themselves. On the whole, I refrained from making cross-references to other works without quoting from them (this the reader/scholar can do in the margin) as the main intention is to induce students and readers to engage directly with literary text. Teachers can use the German-language prose and lyrical texts as translation exercises to add a linguistic element to the historical dimension. The margins can be used for this purpose also. With regard to my choice of texts, the readers might well find other texts more illuminating or fitting to the topic (what about Thomas Bernhard's *Heldenplatz* or Heinz R. Unger's trilogy *Die Republik des Vergessens*, for instance?[iv]) and other historical aspects more telling, in which case they are invited to use the limited space at their disposal to make those points. The main thing is that they should observe the workbook as a facilitator rather than a definitive statement and, above all, that they involve themselves in the discussion. It is my greatest wish that this book should be for some a voyage of discovery that inspires them to seek out and acquaint themselves with the original texts of this remarkable literature in their entirety.

Eoin Bourke

National University of Ireland, Galway
December 2000

Notes

[i]   Hans Mayer, *Ein Deutscher auf Widerruf. Erinnerungen*, vol. I, Frankfurt a.M., 1988, p. 205.

[ii]   Heinrich Heine, *Sämtliche Schriften in zwölf Bänden*, ed. Klaus Briegleb, Munich/Vienna 1976, vol. 3, p. 330.

[iii]   Franz Kain, "... Wie es wirklich gewesen ist ... Vom Literarischen in der heutigen Geschichtsforschung", in Herbert Hummer, Reinhard Kannonier, Brigitte Kepplinger (ed.), *"Die Pflicht zum Widerstand." Festschrift für Peter Kammerstätter zum 75. Geburtstag*, Vienna/Munich/Zurich, 1986, p. 215.

[iv]   Thomas Bernhard, *Heldenplatz*, Frankfurt a.M., 1988; Heinz R. Unger, *Die Republik des Vergessens. Drei Stücke: Unten durch – Zwölfeläuten – Hoch hinaus*, Vienna/Zurich, 1987.

The Austrian Anschluss in History and Literature

1. The events leading to the Anschluss

One tends to think of the twentieth century as the "Age of Democracy" in Europe, and yet from 1936 on there were only three parliamentary democracies to speak of in Central and Southern Europe: Switzerland, Czechoslovakia and, to some extent, Hungary. Mussolini had set the trend towards authoritarian corporatism with his fascist state in 1926; Portugal had been ruled by military cliques since 1926 and by the dictator Salazar since 1932; in Poland an authoritarian constitution replaced the parliamentary system in 1926 under the "guidance" of Josef Pilsudski; in Yugoslavia, King Alexander I dissolved the Belgrade parliament in 1929 and established a dictatorship; Romania was governed as an old-style monarchy by King Carol II since 1930 and as a fascist state from 1938 on; Hitler came to power in January 1933 in Germany and suspended the parliament seven weeks later; in 1936 General Metaxas forced his way to power in Greece by a *coup d'état*, and in the same year the "Caudillo" Franco destroyed the short-lived Second Spanish Republic and became dictator; Hungary, though it had a parliament, was governed from 1932 to 1936 by the ultra-right-winger and anti-Semite Gyula Gömbös.

Austria was no exception to this ominous pattern. The democratically elected Federal Chancellor of the First Republic, Engelbert Dollfuß of the *Christlichsoziale Partei*, suspended the parliament in 1933 and established an ultra-conservative corporative state in which the more radically right-wing Austrian National Socialists as well as the left-wing Social Democrats and the numerically insignificant Communist Party were outlawed and his own *Vaterländische Front* was declared to be the only legal political movement, while its symbol, the *Kruckenkreuz*, a cross-cramponee designed to be suggestive of both a swastika and a Crusaders' cross, was soon to be made the national emblem. The designation "Republic" for Austria was abolished. The death penalty was restored, censorship was introduced, oppositional clubs, newspapers and trade unions were banned, thousands of National Socialists, Social Democrats and Communists were jailed or interned and some of their members even executed. Though modelled on Mussolini's *fascismo*, Dollfuß's *christlich-deutscher Ständestaat* was more similar to the Spanish *Falange* in that it made Catholicism one of its ideological pillars and gave the Church sweeping powers in the areas of education and family law. There was to be no civic divorce. People who demonstratively left the Church risked a six-week prison sentence. From 1936 on, non-religious workers were told they would be sacked if they refused to re-enter the Church. Dollfuß's dictatorship came to be known as Austro-fascism or "clerico-fascism" because the regime was against a pan-Germanic Austrian integration into the Third Reich in rejection of Prussian Protestantism as well as of Nazi anticlericalism rather than due to deep systemic differences. The Austrian élite was also anti-Semitic if less overtly so, a fact which the writer Lili Körber summed up with the observation that, leading up to Christmas, the Austrian Chamber of Commerce staged a campaign with the slogan "Christen, kauft bei Christen!". Körber comments sarcastically: "In Deutschland heißt es einfach: 'Kauft nicht bei Juden', aber wir in Wien sind höfliche Leute".[1]

When Dollfuß was shot dead in an abortive putsch attempt by Austrian Nazis in 1934, he was succeeded by Kurt von Schuschnigg as the head of the unitary state. Many Nazis were arrested and thirteen executed for their participation in the assassination. Schuschnigg at first felt secure in his bid to preserve an independent Catholic Austria because Mussolini had sent troops to the Brenner Pass on the occasion of Dollfuß's assassination, to warn Germany not to intervene in Austrian affairs. To appease Italy, Germany hypocritically dissociated itself from the Austrian Nazi coup attempt (although it had been secretly involved) and even announced that it was closing its borders to fleeing insurrectionists. Germany had had secret plans to annexe Austria since Schuschnigg rescinded the law expelling the Habsburgs on 10 July, 1935, but Hitler now decided to carry out the annexation by "evolutionary" means, i.e. by instructing the Austrian Nazis to infiltrate the "Fatherland Front", government circles, army, police and provincial administrations rather than to attempt another coup. Such an infiltration was made easier by the fact that in certain bureaucratic and academic circles there had always been a tendency to think in semi-mystical pan-Germanic terms.[2] For the Hitler regime the occupation of Austria was considered to be essential, by no means for the overt sentimental reasons as expressed in the loudly proclaimed slogans "Deutsches Blut gehört zusammen" and "Volk will zu Volk", but rather in order to gain direct access to Austria's considerable raw materials and resources which were badly needed for the German arms industry (iron ore, manganese, lead, zinc, antimony, tungsten, copper, magnesite, mineral oil, wood and water power) as well as to secure the southern flank in preparation for an invasion of Czechoslovakia and Poland, all of which was planned long in advance of 1939. In other words, Germany was in effect playing cat and mouse with Austria.

Dollfuß's Austro-fascism was further threatened by Mussolini's speedy *rapprochement* with Hitler from 1935 on. In return for Hitler's non-intervention in Italy's bid to become an imperialist power by invading Abyssinia, his supply of Krupp cannons for the invasion as well as his turning a deaf ear to the wish of the ethnic Germans in South Tyrol to join a future "Großdeutschland", Mussolini obliged Hitler by reneging on his support of Austrian independence. When Schuschnigg realized this, he felt forced to enter upon a pact with Germany, the July Agreement of 1936, which stated that Austria, though independent, was a German state. Schuschnigg increasingly made concessions to the Right, both to the Legitimists, who wanted to revert to pre-Republican conditions by reinstating the Habsburg monarchy, and to the illegal National Socialists. These latter consisted largely of disgruntled members of society that considered themselves deprived of their rightful position in life by Jewish competition, capitalist economics and mass production: unemployed academics, badly paid white-collar workers, students with few prospects, disorientated youth, struggling tradesmen, ex-officers, farmhands, as well as members of the unemployed and sub-proletariat. In compliance with Hitler's wishes, 17,000 Austrian Nazis were given amnesty. On the other hand, Schuschnigg's deeply reactionary sentiments prevented him until literally the last moment from calling upon the only groups that might conceivably have been instrumental in withstanding the Nazi threat or at least forming an effective resistance movement: the worker members and intellectuals of the proscribed Social Democrats, Revolutionary Socialists and Communists.

In June, 1937, Germany used the resurgence of Austrian monarchism as an excuse for the Wehrmacht to work out manœuvres ("Sonderfall Otto", called after Otto von Habsburg, the pretender to the Austrian throne) to practise an invasion of Austria. Economic pressure was placed on Austria to create a monetary and customs union with the Third Reich by withholding German payments for Austrian goods and raw materials and reducing imports by 40%. In November, 1937, Hitler stated *in camera* that, to improve the Reich's military position, Czechoslovakia and Austria had to be subjugated. Hermann Göring spoke openly of an annexation planned for the spring of 1938, predicting correctly that England, France and the Soviet Union would not interfere. On 12 February, 1938, Schuschnigg was summoned to the Berghof in Berchtesgaden, where Hitler set up a fake council of war with three generals to intimidate Schuschnigg:

> Und so eilen Adjutanten und Offiziere mit Hackenknallen, Hitlergruß, Kehrtwendungen, in Stahlhelm und gewichsten Stiefeln, in braunen und schwarzen Uniformen geschäftig über die Marmorböden des Berghofs.[3]

Hitler staged a fit of rage, stamping his foot, screaming at Schuschnigg and deriding his weakness, while comparing himself to an elemental force:

> Ich brauche nur einen Befehl zu geben, und über Nacht ist der ganze lächerliche Spuk an der Grenze zerstoben. Sie werden doch nicht glauben, daß Sie mich auch nur eine halbe Stunde aufhalten können!? Wer weiß – vielleicht bin ich über Nacht einmal in Wien! Wie der Frühlingssturm! Dann sollen Sie etwas erleben![4]

Goebbels wrote into his diary: "Kanonen sprechen immer eine gute Sprache".[5] A journal for political exiles in Paris, *Die Arbeiter-Zeitung*, commented on 1 March:

> Damit Schuschnigg den Sinn dieser Drohung ja nicht mißverstehe, waren während dieses Gespräches auch die Führer der deutschen Wehrmacht in Hitlers Landsitz in Berchtesgaden anwesend. Sie wurden Schuschnigg bei dem Mittagessen vorgeführt. Unter dem Eindruck dieser Drohungen machte Schuschnigg in die Hosen. Er unterwarf sich den Befehlen Hitlers.[6]

Schuschnigg was browbeaten into legalizing the Austrian National Socialists and accepting them into his government, as well as declaring a general amnesty for all Nazi internees and prisoners, even including those who had been involved in the assassination of the party's founder and his own predecessor Dollfuß. On Hitler's insistence, the Austrian general chief of staff Alfred Jansa was forced to resign because he was in favour of military resistance against a German invasion. On hearing of this, the writer Leo Perutz wrote into his diary the words "Finis Austriae".[7] The Nazi Arthur Seyß-Inquart became Minister for the Interior and thus the powerful head of police and security operations, and began immediately to undermine Schuschnigg's authority. In Carinthia, Styria and Upper Austria massive pro-Hitler demonstrations were staged and in Graz the swastika was hoisted on the central square. On 1 March Seyß-Inquart got a rapturous reception there when he officially allowed the wearing of swastikas and the use of the "Sieg Heil" greeting with outstretched right arm, grandly called "der deutsche Gruß". This was followed on 5 March in Linz by his permission to sing the German national anthem and the Horst Wessel song in public. The situation in rural districts was summed up when the police chief of Ried im Innkreis reported on 9 March that almost everyone was wearing a swastika in what amounted to a "Hakenkreuzpsychose" and that among the population "ein außerordentlicher Grußwille durch Heben der rechten Hand" was in evidence.[8] Also on the streets of Vienna the Nazi presence became more and more obtrusive. The German Tourist Office in the centre of the city now displayed a huge portrait of Hitler in the window. Lili Körber wrote:

> Das deutsche Reisebüro in der Kärntnerstraße ist der Wallfahrtsort der Nazi geworden. Elegante Damen pilgern dorthin mit Blumensträußen, die sie vor dem großen Hitlerbild deponieren wie vor einer Madonna. Grüne Jungen patrouillieren davor, provozieren die Passanten. Alle zehn Schritte bieten die Nazikolporteure brüllend ihre Zeitung, den "Volksruf", an.[9]

On the night of 8 March there were clashes in the streets of Vienna between groups of young Nazis and supporters of the "Fatherland Front".

On 9 March Schuschnigg, with unexpected courage, announced in Innsbruck that there would be a plebiscite on Sunday, 13 March, to let the people decide the fate of Austria, ending his speech with Andreas Hofer's historic appeal to his fellow-Tyroleans to withstand Napoleon's invasion of 1809: "Mannder, 's ischt Zeit!" The *Neues Wiener Tagblatt*, the same newspaper that three days later would be transformed into little more than a pro-Nazi propaganda sheet, reported on the "tempestuous and jubilant reception" of Schuschnigg's speech:

> Die Musikkapelle intonierte das Andreas Hofer-Lied, das die Versammelten stehend, mit erhobenem Schwurfinger mitsingen. Anschließend neuerliche tosende Heil-Schuschnigg-Rufe und Ovationen für den Kanzler [...].[10]

Of Thursday, 10 March, Lili Körber wrote that the day began full of hope:

> Durch die Straßen sausten die Reklameautos der Vaterländischen Front und warfen Zettel aus: "Stimmt mit

Ja!" Auch auf den Trottoirs waren große "Ja" neben vaterländischen Kruckenkreuzen mit weißer Farbe gemalt. Aus den Lautsprechern tönten die heiteren altösterreichischen Märsche: "Mir san vom K. und K. Infanterieregiment", der Radetzkymarsch und andere. Vor dem deutschen Reisebüro stand Polizei mit Karabinern. Es herrschte Ruhe".[11]

Schuschnigg was to be heard on radio throughout the country appealing to the people to vote "für ein freies und deutsches, unabhängiges und soziales, für ein christliches und einiges Österreich!", concluding his speech with the emotive words: "[...] die Welt soll unseren Lebenswillen sehen: darum Volk von Österreich, stehe auf wie ein Mann und stimme mit 'Ja'! – Front-Heil! Österreich!"[12] The Leftist groups, though still excluded from political legality, rallied to the cause along with Legitimist, Catholic and Liberal groupings, a factor which made a positive outcome of the plebiscite very likely, had it been allowed to take place on the date announced. A second factor in favour of success was the exclusion of persons under 24 years of age from the plebiscite, in other words, of the age group with the largest potential leaning towards Nazism. Goebbels wrote in his diary:

> Schuschnigg plant einen ganz gemeinen Bubenstreich. Will uns übertölpeln. Ein dummes und albernes Volksbegehren machen. Dazu eine gemeine Rede.[13]

Hitler knew very well of the likely outcome, and therefore ordered Operation Otto to go into action in the early hours of Friday, 11 March. He demanded that the plebiscite be postponed for several weeks and gave orders for an immediate invasion of Austria, supposedly to restore order, protect the "deutschgesinnte Bevölkerung" from acts of violence and prevent further blood-spilling. In fact, no blood had been spilt up to that point. In the course of the morning, Nazi loudspeaker trucks made the intentionally fallacious announcement of Schuschnigg's resignation as a means of spreading confusion. The German radio repeatedly broadcast the news, again fallacious, of a bloody Communist uprising all over Austria. Schuschnigg resigned at 4 p.m. and was replaced as Chancellor on Göring's orders by Seyß-Inquart. At around 5 p.m. news arrived that neither England nor France intended to intervene, upon which the Austrian army was ordered to stay in their barracks during the German invasion, as military resistance was considered hopeless without support from the Western powers. That evening at 7.50 on the Austrian radio Schuschnigg made his farewell speech, in which he replied to the Nazi destabilization tactics thus:

> Ich stelle fest vor der Welt, daß die Nachrichten, die in Österreich verbreitet wurden, daß Arbeiterunruhen gewesen seien, daß Ströme von Blut geflossen seien, daß die Regierung nicht Herrin der Lage wäre und aus Eigenem nicht hätte Ordnung machen können, von A bis Z erfunden sind.[14]

Already under arrest and flanked by two of his own former bodyguards now sporting armbands with swastikas, he ended with the words:

> So verabschiede ich mich in dieser Stunde von dem österreichischen Volk mit einem deutschen Wort und einem Herzenswunsch: Gott schütze Österreich![15]

Mimi Großberg's poem "Weltgeschichte am Radio (12. März 1938)" records the despairing reactions of a Jewish Viennese family listening to Schuschnigg's speech:

> "Gott schütze Österreich!", das war das bitt're
> bedeutungsvolle Abschiedwort des Kanzlers.
> Und, was dann folgte, war zwar Haydns Weise,
> doch schon das Deutschlandlied, nicht Öst'reichs Hymne.
> Wir saßen wie erstarrt am Apparat
> die ganze lange schicksalsschwere Nacht.
>
> Es kam Bericht um furchtbaren Bericht.
> Die Deutschen rückten ein, ganz ohne Schuß,
> man wollte jeden Bruderkampf vermeiden...
> Doch brachten sie, um das Vertrau'n zu sichern,
> Flieger und Tanks in unser kleines Land,
> und drohend durch die Nacht drang dumpfes Dröhnen.
>
> Wie eine Schlange, die die Beute festhält
> mit ihrem lähmend bösen Todesblick,
> so ließ der Apparat uns nicht mehr los.
> Wir hörten auch, wie Österreichs Verräter
> die längst erwarteten Armeen Hitlers
> beim Kanzleramt gigantisch feierten,
> "Sieg Heil, Sieg Heil!" – und das Horst-Wessel-Lied.
>
> "Gott schütze Österreich!" – das kam zu spät.
> In jener Nacht verloren wir die Heimat.[16]

Gerda Hoffer's family also sat around the radio in their house in Grinzing:

> Die Angst war allein nicht auszuhalten. Unsere jüdischen Nachbarn kamen herüber; die Eltern meines Freundes schickten ihn zu uns, um zu hören, ob mein Vater etwas mehr wisse. An diesem Abend hockten wir beieinander, und

es war, als ob wir zur Schiva (Trauer) säßen für den Staat, der einmal Österreich gewesen war.[17]

Also the friends of Ernst and Stella Klaar had gathered in their flat in the Pichlergasse to listen to Schuschnigg's speech. Their son Georg has described the scene in his English-language memoir *Last Waltz in Vienna*:

> They played the national anthem. After the last few bars of Haydn's tune we all sat in utter silence for a few moments. Then, before any of us had had a chance to say anything, the sounds of hundreds of men shouting at the top of their voices could be heard. Still indistinct, still distant, it sounded threatening none the less. Those raucous voices grew louder, were coming closer.
>
> I rushed to the window and looked out into Nussdorferstrasse. It was still quite empty. A few moments. Then the first lorry came into sight. It was packed with shouting, screaming men. A huge swastika flag fluttered over their heads. Most of them had swastika armlets on their sleeves, some wore S.A. caps, some even steel helmets.
>
> Now we could hear clearly what they were shouting: '*Ein Volk, ein Reich, ein Führer!*" they were chanting in chorus, followed by '*Ju-da verr-rrecke! Ju-da verr-rrecke!*' (Perish Judah!). In English this sounds softer, less threatening, but in German, coming from a thousand throats, screaming it out in the full fury of their hate, as lorry after lorry with frenzied Nazis passed below our window, it is a sound one can never forget.[18]

Hans Schauder and a girlfriend Liesel Kampstein were to have an even more surreal experience on that same evening while making their way to a meeting of a group of anthroposophical students of medicine:

> Liesel und ich sind mit der Straßenbahn hingefahren und hatten keine Ahnung, wie schicksalsträchtig dieser Abend für uns werden sollte. Als wir in die Straßenbahn einstiegen, spürten wir sofort eine ungemein bedrückende und gespenstische Atmosphäre. Etwas ganz anderes, vorher noch nie Dagewesenes breitete sich an diesem Abend in dieser Wiener Tram aus. Die Bahn war voll besetzt. Wir beide fanden keinen Platz mehr und standen als einzige im Gang. Alle starrten uns schweigend an. Niemand sprach ein Wort. Und dann sahen wir, daß alle ausnahmslos Hakenkreuze angesteckt hatten. Manche trugen ganz kleine, im letzten Augenblick irgendwo ergatterte, die meisten trugen diese großen "Pletschen", wie wir das nannten. Ich flüsterte mit Liesel, wieso denn das sein konnte, daß nur Hakenkreuzler in der Straßenbahn waren. Keiner um uns sagte ein Wort. Die

vertraute und geschwätzige Tram von gestern war plötzlich in ein uns fremdes und feindseliges Gefährt verwandelt. Die anderen betrachteten uns schweigend, und es war ganz klar, daß sie uns beide, die einzigen ohne Hakenkreuz, für verlorene Kreaturen hielten. Sie wurden in keiner Weise gegen uns aggressiv. Wir wurden nur stumm ausgegrenzt und fühlten uns allein.[19]

The Viennese writer Hilde Spiel, already living in exile in London and following the events over the radio, wrote into her diary: "Es ist gräßlich und unerträglich. Die Eltern sitzen im Feuer. Der Teufel regiert".[20]

The following excerpt from Gitta Sereny's memoirs describing the same evening makes it clear that the "devil" did not only come from without, but rather that the ground was well prepared in Austria for the events that were to come. The 15-year-old Gitta, who was of Hungarian Protestant stock, met up with her friend Elfie on the evening of 11 March at the statue of Mozart in the Stadtpark:

> While I waited for Elfie in the dark, deserted park, I heard for the first time a sound that was to echo around Vienna for weeks: the rhythmic chant of many voices shouting words I had never heard before: 'Deutschland erwache! Juda verrecke!' – Germany awake! Jewry perish!
> When Elfie arrived we stood stiffly in the darkness listening. Then she said, "My father – "
> "What's the matter with your father?" I asked, and then, to my own surprise, added, "Is he a Jew?"
> Elfie looked at me helplessly. "A Jew?" she said, confused, her voice tight. "He is a Nazi. They told me tonight. He's been an illegal for years. He said I was never to speak to any Jews in school, and that anyway" – her voice sounded dead – "the whole place will be ... disinfected from top to bottom. What shall I do?" She sobbed, holding on to me. "How can I not talk to Jews?" Then, for the first time, she put into words the subject that had never touched us, reeling off the names of four of our teachers [at the Max Reinhardt Drama School] whose criticism or praise had dominated our lives for over a year.
> I was almost speechless. "But why?" I asked, and then, immediately, "How do you know they are Jewish?"
> "He knows" she said, tonelessly. "He says they are Saujuden and they will all be got rid of".
> "Got rid of?" I repeated stupidly, and she cried out then, furiously, "Didn't you hear what I said? Disinfected, he calls it, the schools, the theatres, everywhere" – she spat out the word – "disinfected". The chanting from the street went on and on as we stood there under the trees.[21]

Hardly had Schuschnigg spoken his last words when Vienna was to witness the most extraordinary scenes since the violent suppression of labour demonstrations in July, 1927, or the smashing of the Left by government forces in 1934. The surgeon Dr Willy Stern reminisces:

> Die Stadt war wie verwandelt. Wo sich auf dem Weg zu meinem Onkel ein alltägliches, normal zivilisiertes Bild dargeboten hatte, waren nun plötzlich Menschenmassen auf den Straßen, die aus den Seitengassen in die Hauptstraßen quollen: grölende, wie aus der Faschiermaschine quellende, Hakenkreuzbinden tragende, Hakenkreuzfahnen schwingende, Sieg-Heil brüllende, entfesselte Massen! Wir suchten unseren Weg durch Seitengassen, um ungeschoren davonzukommen.[21]

Franz Werfel, a personal friend of Schuschnigg's, described the crudeness of the events in Vienna's inner city with particular bitterness:

> Bereits an der Ecke des Grabens begann das Bild sich zu verändern. Dort standen viele einzelne Menschengruppen, schreiend, fuchtelnd. Plötzlich rasten Automobile vorbei in gottverbotenem Tempo. In den Wagen ragten Männer, die unverständliche Worte ins Leere brüllten. [...] Und nun brach er los, der Mordsgesang, der nur aus zwei Tönen besteht: "Sieg-Heil! Sieg-Heil! Sieg-Heil!" Wie das i-ah eines automatischen Esels von Bergesgröße! Wie das Kriegsgeheul der Steinzeit, mechanisiert im Weltalter der Industrie.[22]

Two things were conspicuous: a linguistic element in the conquest of Werfel's beloved Vienna, that is, a new Prussian tone in the slogans and orders being barked out, and the youthfulness of the crowd, many of them bussed in purposely from the outlying regions:

> Lange Reihen von Autobussen und Lastwagen kamen angerattert, aus denen Hunderte von Weißstrümpfen sich in die Menge herabstürzten. Viele trugen schon Armbinden mit Hakenkreuzen. Junge Burschen waren's, Halbwüchsige zumeist, die man aus den Städten der Bannmeile, aus Mödling, Baden, Bruck, Eisenstadt, Fischamend, Sankt Pölten in die eroberte Metropole geworfen hatte. "Da sind die Korsettstangen", hörte ich jemand sagen, ein preußischer Ausdruck, wildfremd für Wiener Ohren. Schon lagerte dieser neudeutsche Sprachdunst atemberaubend über dem anmutigen Dialekt unsrer Heimat. Die Sieger schoben die Menge sinnlos durcheinander. Ordnungsdienst hieß das. Einige schwangen Gewehre, Knüppel, Stahlruten. Auf ihren glatten oder flaumigen Kindergesichtern brannte eine somnambule Trunkenheit, die ein gewaltigerer Wein erzeugt hatte als der liebe Heurige dieses Landes.[23]

Lili Körber made similar observations:

> Einige Male fuhren Lastautos mit Kindern, Jugendlichen und
> Schupo brüllend und winkend an uns vorbei. Einmal trugen
> die Insassen auch Arbeitskittel, vermutlich hatten sich SA-
> Leute als Arbeiter kostümiert. [...]
>
> Überall schneidiges deutsches Militär; die scharfe
> reichsdeutsche Sprache übertönt unseren weichen Dialekt
> mit dem melodischen romanischen Einschlag.[24]

The reporter Robert Breuer was in the Spiegelgasse at the
time:

> Die Menge war wie berauscht und behext. Alle
> *Vaterländische-Front*-Abzeichen waren gegen das Hakenkreuz
> umgetauscht worden. Die Polizei, die gestern noch versucht
> hatte, die Nazis abzudrängen, erschien mit Haken-
> kreuzschleifen als Armbinden und wurde mit erhobener
> Rechter und lauten Rufen "Heil Polizei!" begrüßt. Durch die
> schreiende, kreischende, tobende Menge bahnten sich
> mühsam Automobile den Weg, in denen Unterführer und
> Unterunterführer standen, welche die Menge mit dem Hitler-
> Gruß grüßten.[25]

Over and over again eye-witnesses used the metaphors of the
Witches' Sabbath and Fasching to depict the street scenes
that greeted them, such as G.E.R. Geyde:

> Es war ein unbeschreiblicher Hexensabbat – Sturmtrupp-
> leute, von denen viele kaum der Schulbank entwachsen
> waren, marschierten mit umgeschnalltem Patronengürtel und
> Karabinern, als einziges Zeichen ihrer Autorität
> die Hakenkreuzbinde auf dem Ärmel, neben Überläufern aus den
> Reihen der Polizei; Männer und Frauen brüllten und schrien
> hysterisch den Namen ihres Führers, umarmten die
> Wachleute und zogen sie mit sich in den wirbelnden
> Menschenstrom [...].[26]

Or Gregor von Rezzori:

> Die Nacht war in einem Taumel der Begeisterung vergangen,
> mahlend im dumpfen Rhythmus ihrer Tritte, hatten die
> schweigend marschierenden Blocks der Dunkelmänner
> schließlich die Fastnacht ausgelöst, Menschen strömten
> plötzlich aus den Häusern in die Straßen und schlossen sich
> den stummen Kolonnen an, umtanzten sie in Ekstase,
> jubelnd, jauchzend, Fahnen schwenkend, einander um-
> armend, hüpfend, schreiend, schäumend in Delirium.[27]

Carl Zuckmayer explained the preponderance of youth as a
special measure to give a dynamic edge to the takeover:

Die Atmosphäre in Wien war sehr merkwürdig in diesen Vorfrühlingstagen. Äußerlich hatte sie etwas von einem Fastnachtstreiben. Denn die Leitung der Nazipartei hatte von Deutschland aus einen unerhört raffinierten Befehl erhalten: Kinder auf die Straße! Erwachsene bleiben daheim.[28]

Various observers recorded a further phenomenon which they could not quite explain: the fact that the faces of the Viennese now filling the streets had changed. "Nie sah ich", wrote Walter Mehring, "solche Wandlungen von Physiognomien, nicht einmal in Berlins letzten Tagen. Der Hunneneinbruch, der Türkensturm konnte nicht verfremdender gewesen sein".[29] Friedrich Torberg observed:

Tatsächlich: es sind andre Gesichter. Tatsächlich: es sind andre Menschen. Nicht bloß veränderte, nicht bloß verwandelte, nein: andre. Und nicht bloß jene, deren Fremdheit schon äußerlich sich kundtut, durch Gewand und Gehaben und Sprache – nein, auch die unverkennbar der Stadt Entstammten. [...] Lauter Türlschnapper. Die eilfertig sonst bereitstanden und spähten, ob sie nicht einen Wagenschlag öffnen könnten und dafür ein Trinkgeld beanspruchen – jetzt sind sie ihres Anspruchs gewiß, jetzt hat ihre plumpe, plebejische Servilität sich in ein plumpes, plebejisches Gegenteil verkehrt, jetzt warten sie nicht darauf, eine ungebetene Dienstleistung anzubringen, sondern sie schweifen umher und bestimmen sich selbst die Beute, suchen sich selbst ihre Opfer aus, jetzt ist ihr Geducktsein kein dienstbereites mehr sondern ein räuberisches, frech zur Schau tragen sie ihr Recht auf den Raub, und werden es anmelden, wann es ihnen beliebt [...].[30]

These remarks are not only a comment on the political fickleness of the sub-proletariat, as already observed long before by Marx and Engels,[31] but have a very topical dimension relating to those early days of the Anschluss. Carl Zuckmayer explained it in terms of a destabilization tactic contrived by the Nazis by paying beggars and down-and-outs a small pocket-money to invade the elegant inner city on that day:

Eine ähnliche Zerfallserscheinung, in Wahrheit ein geplanter Trick der Umstürzler, war das maßlose Anschwellen der Bettlerscharen, die – in kleinerem Ausmaß – schon vorher in der Hauptstadt ein Problem waren. Jetzt bekamen sie, wie man später erfuhr, von der illegalen Partei ein Tagesgeld, wenn sie in möglichst jammervollem und zerlumptem Zustand besonders die noble, von Ausländern bevorzugte Innenstadt, den ersten Bezirk zwischen Ring, Kärntner Straße, Stephansplatz, Graben, Kohlmarkt, massenweise bevölkerten und die Passanten beunruhigten. Offenbar hatten die Nazis etwas aus der 'Dreigroschenoper' gelernt.[32]

Zuckmayer, an eye-witness also of the events in the night of 11–12 March, described the pandemonium that resulted from the engineered flooding of the city with unsavoury elements in terms of a medieval vision of Hell:

> An diesem Abend brach die Hölle los. Die Unterwelt hatte ihre Pforten aufgetan und ihre niedrigsten, scheußlichsten, unreinsten Geister losgelassen. Die Stadt verwandelte sich in ein Alptraumgemälde des Hieronymus Bosch: Lemuren und Halbdämonen schienen aus Schmutzeiern gekrochen und aus versumpften Erdlöchern gestiegen. Die Luft war von einem unablässig gellenden, wüsten, hysterischen Gekreische erfüllt, aus Männer– und Weiberkehlen, das tage– und nächtelang weiterschrillte. Und alle Menschen verloren ihr Gesicht, glichen verzerrten Fratzen: die einen in Angst, die andren in Lüge, die andren in wildem, haßerfülltem Triumph. [...] Hier war nichts losgelassen als die dumpfe Masse, die blinde Zerstörungswut, und ihr Haß richtete sich gegen alles durch Natur und Geist Veredelte. Es war ein Hexensabbat des Pöbels und ein Begräbnis aller menschlichen Würde.[33]

At 9.45 p.m. on 11 March, Göring gave the order that Seyß-Inquart was to close the Austrian borders, "damit die da [die Juden] nicht mit dem Vermögen abschieben".[34] At 10.45 p.m. Hitler was assured over the telephone by his envoy in Rome that Mussolini agreed to the Anschluss, at which Hitler effused:

> Dann sagen Sie bitte Mussolini, ich werde ihm dies nie vergessen! Nie, nie, nie, was immer geschehen mag. [...] Sobald die österreichische Angelegenheit geregelt ist, werde ich bereit sein, durch dick und dünn mit ihm zu gehen.[35]

In the early hours of the morning of Saturday, 12 March, and in advance of the German army's entry into Austria at 8 a.m., Heinrich Himmler and Reinhard Heydrich arrived in Vienna with a contingent of Gestapo to supervise the arrest and, in some cases, the murder of non-Nazi politicians, functionaries, socialists and Jewish leaders. Of the Municipal Fire Brigade alone, 54 members were to be executed, given life sentences or deported. The attaché Wilhelm von Ketteler in the German Embassy, who sympathized with Austrian independence, was fetched that day and brought in a car to Modena Park in the centre of the city, where he was bludgeoned to death. His corpse, with shattered skull, was fished out of the Danube on March 15 just as Hitler was making his Heldenplatz speech.

The subalterns of the Nazi movement who had felt the brunt of the authoritarian Schuschnigg regime now had a field-day. When Minister Eduard Ludwig was questioned by a prison warder as to his profession and answered "Leiter des Bundespressedienstes", the warder slapped him across the face and said, "Das warst du. Jetzt bist du ein Stück Scheiße, merk dir das!"[36] Within a few weeks 70,000 persons were taken prisoner and many of them executed. Schuschnigg was placed under house arrest for ten weeks, which were followed by seven years in "preventive detention" and various concentration camps. Among those arrested was Dr Loebel, the editor-in-chief of the liberal *Neues Wiener Tagblatt*. Subsequently, the same newspaper, now under new management and with its subtitle "Demokratisches Organ" deleted, reported favourably on the purge in the stilted, pseudo-legalistic rhetoric of Nazism:

> Die personelle Säuberung der österreichischen Polizei wurde sofort nach dem Muster des Reiches auf Grund des Reichsgesetzes zur Wiederherstellung des Beamtentums in Angriff genommen. Alle politisch unzuverlässigen Beamten und Offiziere wurden, sofern sie nicht schon in Schutzhaft genommen wurden, ihres Dienstes enthoben und einstweilen beurlaubt.[37]

As Ernst Lothar put it: "Dieselben Zeitungen, die noch gestern Schuschnigg in den Himmel gehoben hatten, spien ihn heute an".[38] The fundamental change of tone in the Viennese press was due to the fact that planeloads of "Aryan" journalists had been flown into Vienna to replace the largely Jewish editorial boards. Also the street scene had changed radically, as depicted by Lili Körber:

> Der scharfe Frühjahrswind fegte die letzten Zettel empor aus den Papierfluten, die gestern noch die Straßen überschwemmten: "Mit Schuschnigg für Österreich!" Die schweren Stiefel der SA-Truppen, die von allen Seiten anmarschiert kamen, traten über sie hinweg. Mit ihren Fahnen und Wimpeln, in Dreier-, Vierer- und Sechserreihen nahmen sie die ganze Straße ein. Die Kruckenkreuzfahnen sind verschwunden. Wo man hinblickt – das Hakenkreuz auf rotem Feld.[39]

The 21-year-old medical student Stella Sigmann (later the poet Stella Rotenberg) divined not only an atmosphere of elation but also an admixture of cravenness:

> On Saturday morning it was very cold and very fine and clear. They called it "Hitler weather," just as before World War One there was "Emperor's weather". The streets were crowded.

People were quite different, as if aroused. Everyone was excited – joyfully excited and yet somehow anxious. I entered a shop, and there was a man next to me who said, "Why don't you come and have a cup of coffee with me," or something of the kind. I declined with thanks: "No, no, thank you, I am Jewish!" Whereupon he said: "Oh, I can't believe that!" And I said, "But yes, I am Jewish!" Then he looked at me and suddenly I saw that he was frightened – and that on a day when the German troops had not yet entered Vienna. But already he was frightened. So I thought, Good God, this place is a prison already! People were frightened to be seen with a Jew: "racial defilement".[40]

A proclamation of Hitler's was read out in the radio by Goebbels at midday, renaming Austria "Deutschösterreich":

Seit heute morgen marschieren über alle Grenzen Deutschösterreichs die Soldaten der Deutschen Wehrmacht. Panzertruppen, Infanteriedivisionen und die SS-Verbände auf der Erde und die deutsche Luftwaffe im blauen Himmel werden, selbst gerufen von der neuen nationalsozialistischen Regierung in Wien, der Garant dafür sein, daß dem österreichischen Volk nunmehr endlich in kürzester Frist die Möglichkeit geboten wird, durch eine wirkliche Volksabstimmung seine Zukunft und damit sein Schicksal selbst zu gestalten.[41]

Although the invasion was in contravention of international law, the Treaties of Saint-Germain and Versailles as well as the July Agreement of 1936, the only country in the world to lodge a formal veto with the League of Nations was Mexico. As the historian Helmut Andics put it:

Die Patentdemokraten im Westen, die Briten und Franzosen, hatten keinen Finger krumm gemacht, um Österreich zu retten. Im Gegenteil: Sie zeigten sich deutlich bemüht, Hitler bei guter Laune zu halten. Sie hatten sich ganz offensichtlich mit dem deutschen Führer und seinen Methoden abgefunden, sie verurteilten sein Vorgehen nicht, sie tauschten Botschafter mit ihm aus, und schlossen Verträge; sie dachten nicht einmal daran, ihn und sein Deutschland zu boykottieren [...].[42]

Klaus Mann wrote sarcastically of the events of the previous month and days:

Der Bundeskanzler tat die schauerliche Fahrt nach Berchtesgaden; das Plebiszit, das die Nazis erledigen sollte, ward kühn beschlossen – und abgesagt. [...]

Nur die deutsche Armee marschierte, während die italienische sich durchaus still verhielt. Österreich wehrte sich nicht, Frankreich hatte Kabinettskrise, Europa beobachtete mit ehrfurchtsvoller Spannung die historischen Vorgänge, der Führer und der Duce wechselten fröhliche Telegramme.[43]

The fascist newspaper *Das kleine Volksblatt* reported in the mendacious style which was from then on to characterize the media, presenting the invasion as a "goodwill visit":

Heute 8 Uhr morgens haben deutsche motorisierte Truppen die deutschösterreichische Grenze zu einem Freundschafts-besuch überschritten. Zum Zeichen dieses frohen Ereignisses, das von allen Deutschen Österreichs begeistert begrüßt wird, flaggt alles.[44]

At 3.50 p.m. Hitler arrived at Braunau to pay a carefully choreographed visit to his parents' grave (for the last time in his life) and continued on to Linz. According to Goebbels' diary, the events of the day brought tears to his eyes:

Die Juden sind größtenteils geflüchtet. Wohin? Als ewige Juden ins Nichts. Der Führer ist in Österreich eingetroffen. Mit unbeschreiblichem Jubel in Braunau begrüßt. Er ist auf der Fahrt nach Linz und will noch weiter bis Wien. Das wird ein Einzug sein. Ich bin so glücklich.[45]

Hitler's approach to Linz was staged so as to resemble Advent, the coming of the Saviour. The 17-year-old Erich Fried was listening in to the radio that day and later described the false piety of the occasion and the uncanny irony of the drunken broadcasters' *faux-pas*:

Jetzt hörten wir eine Übertragung aus Linz, der Hauptstadt Oberösterreichs, die den feierlichen Einzug des Führers Adolf Hitler erwartete. Die Männer am Mikrophon, zum Teil ortsbekannte Nazigrößen, hatten Ausblick auf einen großen Platz, auf dem Hitlerjugend und BDM-Mädchen versammelt waren, sowie Tausende von Schaulustigen. Sie teilten uns mit, daß in den Fenstern der meisten Häuser schon Kerzen bereitstünden, um beim Nahen des Führers angezündet zu werden, daß sich aber die Ankunft des Führers verzögert habe. Es sei kalt und alle könnten es vor Ungeduld kaum noch erwarten.

Die Tatsache, daß einige der Nazigrößen offenbar reichlich getrunken hatten, verlieh der Berichterstattung eine eigentümliche Note. So rief einer: "Es ist kalt. Die nackerten Knie der Hitlerjugend wackeln im Wind". Daran schloß er die ermunternde Aufforderung an die Hitlerjugend: "So, jetzt singen wir noch das Lied von den morschen Knochen". Es ging aber keineswegs um die Knochen in den frierenden Beinen der Hitlerjungen, sondern das Lied, das nun erklang, lautete:

"Es zittern die morschen Knochen
der Welt vor dem roten Krieg.
Wir haben den Schrecken gebrochen
und für uns wars ein mächtiger Sieg.

Wir werden weitermarschieren
und wenn alles in Scherben fällt
denn heut gehört uns Deutschland
und morgen die ganze Welt".

Die letzten zwei Zeilen wurden wiederholt. Der eigentliche
Text, verfaßt von einem Hitlerjungen namens Baumann,
lautete zwar: "Denn heute hört uns Deutschland", aber die
Nazis hatten sich diese Worte schon zurechtgesungen. Ich
hörte sie damals zum ersten Mal und habe sie nie wieder
vergessen. [...]

Mittlerweile war es soweit: die betrunkene Stimme am
Mikrophon brüllte: "Der Führer ist im Anrollen! Alle Häuser
anzünden!" Sie meinte allerdings nicht, daß Linz sich selbst
verwüsten solle. Der Mann hatte nur sagen wollen: "Alle
Kerzen anzünden", war aber nicht nüchtern genug.[46]

From the balcony of the town hall on the main square of Linz
Hitler proclaimed in messianic terms to the frenetic cheers of
the townspeople:

Wenn die Vorsehung mich einst aus dieser Stadt heraus zur
Führung des Reiches berief, dann muß sie mir damit einen
Auftrag erteilt haben, und es kann nur ein Auftrag gewesen
sein, meine teure Heimat dem Deutschen Reich wieder-
zugeben".[47]

Austria's right-wing poets answered in kind. Josef Weinheber,
about whom it was later to be claimed that he considered the
Anschluss to be a catastrophe,[48] wrote the following lines in
his cloying "Hymnus an die Wiederkehr":

Nein, noch fassen wir's nicht.
Hatten wir doch zu lang
Vaterland nur im Traum.
Nun aber Bruderhand
liegt in der Bruderhand,
laßt uns schwören den Schwur:
Nie mehr werde getrennt
weises von wachem Blut,
nie mehr stilleres Herz
von der gestählten Stirn,
Himmel von Himmel nicht
und nicht Träne von Trän'.

[...]

Hüben und drüben nicht,
nicht mehr Süden noch Nord:
Wie nur Liebenden, in
seligem Ausgleich, schenkt

Gott ein Lebendes neu:
Hauses Hoffnung und Heil...

Dies im Namen des Volks!
Dies im Namen des Bluts!
Dies im Namen des Leids:

Deutschland, ewig und groß,
Deutschland, wir grüßen dich!
Führer, heilig und stark,
Führer, wir grüßen dich!
Heimat, glücklich und frei,
Heimat, wir grüßen dich![49]

Gertrud Fussenegger, celebrated to this day as one of Austria's foremost writers, outdid Weinheber in rhetorical flatulence in her "Stimme der Ostmark", dated 12 March 1938:

[...]

da war, daß einer erschien,
Deutschlands gültigstes Inbild,
den in dunkelnder Ahnung,
doch weise, frühe Geschlechter
als Retter des Reichs
in dämmernder Zukunft gewahrten,
den sie in schwelenden Sagen
schaudernd gerufen am Abend
blutig verlorener Schlachten,

doch den mit Augen zu schauen
heute uns endlich gegeben –

Er kam im Namen des Reiches,
der vollen Gewalt, des Anspruchs,
der trotzig ehernen Stärke.
Kam, und über ihm flammte
das Zeichen Deutschlands, und schwertgleich
verzehrend Gesetz und Verpflichtung.

Betend wallt' ihm entgegen
freudeweinendes Volk,
sich selbst als Gabe zu ringen,
gewillt zu größtem Bekenntnis. [...][50]

Other effusions written on the same occasion unwittingly reveal both the necromaniacal nature and the sado-masochistic structure of fascism, as in Josef Friedrich

Perkonig's lines from "Die Heimkehr": "Deutschland, du unsere Wiege, / Deutschland, du unser Sarg",[51] or Paul Anton Keller's "Ruf aus der Ostmark. Geschrieben in der Nacht vom 12. zum 13. März 1938":

> Herrliche Freude: Frucht sein am Stamme.
> Herrlicher dies noch: für ihn zu fallen.
> Deutschland! auffunkelnd flutet der Name
> im Geiste, blutesgleich leibhin![52]

And on 13 March, Herbert Strutz works himself up to a homo-erotic declaration of love to Hitler in his poem "Deutsche Heimkehr":

> Schöner und stolzer, als wir dich jemals geglaubt,
> nimmst du uns an, unser Kämpfen und innerstes Sein,
> segnest uns Herzen und Seelen, uns Hände und Haupt,
> und wir sind dein.[53]

On that same Sunday, the psychological warfare was stepped up and the impression of turbulence and threat greatly intensified by the sight and sound of low-flying German bombers over the city of Vienna. Carl Zuckmayer described the atmosphere thus:

> Den ganzen Tag hindurch donnerten die Motoren. Geschwader kreisten unablässig über der Stadt, niedrig, wie zornige Hornissen. Mit dem Geschrei von den Straßen und dem Brüllen der Lautsprecher, die Hitlers letzte Kundgebungen bis zur Erschlaffung wiederholten, mit dem sogenannten 'Sägen', "Sssieg-Heil, Sssieg-Heil, Sssieg-Heil", das pausenlos, aus schon heisergeschrienen Kehlen, die Stadt durchzischte, ergab das einen unsagbar enervierenden, wahrhaft teuflischen Lärm. Man empfand das nicht mehr als menschliche Laute oder technische Geräusche. Das Getöse des Weltuntergangs durchhallte die Luft.[54]

As Friedrich Torberg observed, the noise of the heavy bombers incited the mob to outdo it with mindless screaming. Torberg attempts to reproduce the processes of mass psychology, the ritualistic chanting culminating in the equation of noise with power:

> Aber wir, wir machen ja *auch* Lärm. Hei was für Lärm wir machen, hei, heißah, heil, Siegheil, Heil Hitler, ein Volk ein Reich ein Führer, wir danken unsrem Führer, Heil Hitler, heißah, hei. Solchen Lärm machen wir. Wenn einer mittendrin steht, hört er den Lärm der Flugzeuge gar nicht mehr, und wenn er vollends noch mitbrüllt, mag er fast glauben, daß er stärker sei als die Flugzeuge. So gewaltig ist der Lärm, so mächtig. Lärm ist Macht.[55]

While what amounted to a psychopathological epidemic ruled the streets of Vienna, the Ministerial Council passed a law declaring Austria to be a country of the German Reich, rose from their seats and made the Hitler salute. At the same session, the Austrian army was subsumed by the Wehrmacht, the "Fatherland Front" dissolved and its financial resources taken over in their entirety by the National Socialist party. The same night Gestapo, SS- and SA-men broke into hundreds of Jewish homes, stole cash and expropriated jewellery, precious metals, *objets d'art*, paintings and carpets, the more valuable pieces being delivered by order of the Führer to the Reich Security Headquarters in Berlin. (The collection of paintings belonging to the Jewish brewers Ignaz and Jakob Kuffner of Ottakring were eventually to become Hitler's personal property).

Next day, while Hitler was having his breakfast in the Hotel Weinzinger in the centre of Linz, two *Vaterlandsfront* detectives were strangled in the city jail and two police superintendents were beaten to death in the streets. Now, the very blood the spilling of which the German invasion was allegedly to prevent had begun to spatter the pavements. Hitler and his entourage set off in convoy to Vienna where they received a rousing ecclesiastical welcome: Cardinal Innitzer had ordered all church towers to be festooned with swastikas and church bells to be rung. The Catholic Church, hitherto one of the mainstays and principal beneficiaries of Austro-fascism, did an about-turn. Besides the well-known Nazi slogans like "Ein Volk, ein Reich, ein Führer!", a new chant in Viennese dialect was to be heard in the streets: "Der Kuart ist fuart, nun geht's uns guat!", meaning, since Kurt Schuschnigg is gone, things are going well for us. Seyß-Inquart was now named "Reichsstatthalter", as the title "Bundeskanzler" would have been too suggestive of independence. The *Völkischer Beobachter*, reporting on the events of Monday, 14 March, waxed eloquent in the nauseatingly gushing style peculiar to itself, depicting, as usual, the masses as a malleable fluidum, and Hitler as the rock around which the waves of mere humanity swirl:

> Adolf Hitler, der Führer des Großdeutschen Reiches, hat am Montag nachmittag, kurz nach 17 Uhr, von Linz kommend, die Stadtgrenze Wiens überschritten. Die Millionen Volksgenossen der südlichen Metropole bereiteten dem Führer und Reichskanzler einen triumphalen Empfang, dessen Kundgebungen sich steigerten von der Bannmeile bis ins Zentrum der glücklichen Stadt. Soweit Worte schildern können, sollen sie die großen Eindrücke dieser Stunden zu

schildern versuchen. Der Aufmarsch der Massen, der kurz vor Mittag begann, steigerte sich zwischen 13, 14, 15 und 16 Uhr zu einem unübersichtlichen Getriebe. Die ganze Stadt war wie ein Vulkan, und jeder Stadtteil glich einem Krater, der alle Minuten tausend Menschen ausspie. Die Mariahilferstraße, der Ballhausplatz und der Ring sind eine einzige Menschenflut, die erst verebbt in den westlichen Ausläufern Wiens. [...] Jungvolk zieht in Sechserreihen an die freigehaltenen Plätze. Schulen treten geschlossen an. An dem blaugrauen, sonnenerfüllten Frühlingshimmel sieht man die Geschwader der deutschen Luftwaffe... Eine Viertelstunde später kommt aus dem Westen herauf eine Woge des Jubels. Heilrufe eilen einer riesigen Wagenkolonne voran, und dann biegt um die Ecke der erste Wagen eines endlosen Zuges. Dann folgt der zweite Wagen, und im dritten Wagen steht aufrecht der Führer und grüßt lachenden Auges die Spaliere, die sich vor Begeisterung kaum noch halten können. [...] Nun ist der Führer gekommen. Nun hat er dieses Volk befreit. Er hat ihm nicht nur den Glauben an die Zukunft wiedergegeben, sondern ihm zugleich den uralten Traum, die uralte Sehnsucht erfüllt, Deutsche unter Deutschen zu sein, Deutsche in einem einzigen großdeutschen Reich.[56]

Friedrich Torberg described Hitler's reception in Vienna in terms of a corybantic orgy in which the mob prostrates itself before the false god: L 198354

Und es geschah des großen Höllenreigens letzte Steigerung. Er überschlug sich seinem Gipfel zu, kippte noch ein Mal schrill empor, in einer rasenden Begier sich selbst zu übertreffen, hinauszutorkeln über sich um eines endlich erkennbaren, endlich sichtbaren Sinnes willen: der Herr und Meister erschien, der Leibhaftige hielt seinen Einzug.

[...] Sie tobten und brüllten ihm zu, mit der letzten Kraft ihrer heiseren Kehlen – aber weil sie doch genau so gut jedem andern zugebrüllt hätten, der ihnen nun erschienen wäre, ließen sie willig und erleichtert ihr Gebrüll in vorgeschriebene Texte lenken, in Sprüche und Chöre von erprobtem Wortlaut, und brüllten so diesem Einen zu, als gäbe es wirklich keinen andern, nur ihn, den Führer, den Meister, den Heilbringer, den Hitler, den der gemeint war wenn man Heil Hitler brüllte, heil, Siegheil, Heilhitler, wir danken unserm Führer, wir wollen unseren Führer sehn, lieber Führer sei so nett und zeige dich am Fensterbrett, Heilhitler, Siegheil, heil ...[57]

2. Heldenplatz, 15 March

Shortly after 11 a.m. on Tuesday, 15 March, Hitler held his famous speech to 200,000 people on the Heldenplatz. He who in his youth had been rejected twice by the Viennese Academy of Fine Arts as inadequate and had spent months in a home for down-and-outs was now the focus of the entire nation. In her memoirs, Minna Lachs pondered on what this former lumpen proletarian must have felt on seeing his most megalomaniacal phantasies come true:

> Was muß dieser vom Cäsarenwahn erfüllte Mann, der in jungen Jahren verlachte Arbeitslose, der in dem Männerheim in der Meldemannstraße in Wien gehaust hatte, dem nie etwas gelang, empfunden haben, als er seine phantastischesten Wunschträume als grandiose Wirklichkeit erleben konnte. Was mußte er nach seinem triumphalen Einmarsch in Österreich bei der Kundgebung am 15. März auf dem repräsentativsten und schönsten Platz Wiens, dem Heldenplatz, vor den jubelnden Menschenmassen, vor den Hunderttausenden, die sich an ihrem eigenen Freudentaumel berauschten, empfunden haben![58]

The very name of the venue contributed to the myth-making. With their unfailing sense of theatricality and the æstheticization of political acts, the Nazis could not have chosen a better backdrop, with the sweep of the Outer Burghof's huge concave colonnades on either side of the speaker's gallery, as well as its massive equestrian statues of heroes of bygone days: "Prinz Eugen, der edle Ritter", who saved Vienna from the Turks, and Archduke Carl, who helped to defeat Napoleon at the battle of Aspern, facing each other across the square on colossal steeds dramatically rearing. Hitler cleverly worked the theme of the Austrian repulsion of long past Turkish invasions into his speech as a barely concealed metaphor for the need to repel the Slavic hordes in preparation of the millennial future, while omitting to mention Prince Eugene, who, after all, was a Frenchman. Hitler also carefully underplayed the concept "Österreich" throughout the speech and instead hammered home the attribute "deutsch", using the former only twice in his speech and the latter 16 times. "Österreich" was soon to be eliminated from the Nazi vocabulary as too reminiscent of Austrian independence and replaced by "Ostmark". (Even this term would later be replaced by "Donau- und

Alpengauen", because the first syllable of "Ostmark" was felt to be too evocative of "Österreich".) The excerpts from Hitler's speech as printed in the *Neues Wiener Abendblatt* of 15 March are telling in that they reproduce the audience reaction:

> Ich proklamiere nunmehr für dieses Land seine neue Mission. Sie entspricht dem Gebot, das einst die deutschen Siedler aus allen Gauen des alten Reiches hierhergerufen hat. Die älteste Ostmark des deutschen Volkes soll von nun an das jüngste Bollwerk der deutschen Nation und damit des Deutschen Reiches sein. (*Brausende Sieg-Heil-Rufe.*) Jahrhundertelang haben sich in den unruhevollen Zeiten der Vergangenheit die Stürme des Ostens an den Grenzen der alten Mark gebrochen. Jahrhundertelang für alle Zukunft soll sie nunmehr wieder sein ein eiserner Garant für die Sicherheit und für die Freiheit des Deutschen Reiches. (*Brausende Zustimmung.*) Und damit ein Unterpfand für das Glück und für den Frieden unseres großen Volkes. Ich kann somit in dieser Stunde dem deutschen Volke die größte Vollzugsmeldung meines Lebens abstatten. (*Minutenlanger, brausender Beifall.*) Als Führer und Kanzler der deutschen Nation und des Deutschen Reiches melde ich vor der deutschen Geschichte nunmehr den Eintritt meiner Heimat in das Deutsche Reich. (*Neuerlicher tosender Beifallssturm und Rufe: Heil dem Führer, wir danken unserm Führer.*)[59]

2.1 Ernst Jandl's literarization of the event

In the crowd on that day, the twelve-year-old Ernst Jandl was wedged between grown-ups on the Ringstraße near Heldenplatz.[60] Twenty-four years later, in June 1962, he was to write this bizarre text in recollection of the equally bizarre event:

wien: heldenplatz

der glanze heldenplatz zirka
versaggerte in maschenhaftem männchenmeere
drunter auch frauen die ans maskelknie
zu heften heftig sich versuchten, hoffensdick.
und brüllzten wesentlich.

verwogener stirnscheitelunterschwang
nach nöten nördlich, kechelte
mit zu-nummernder aufs bluten feilzer stimme
hinsensend sämmertliche eigenwäscher.

pirsch!
döppelte der gottelbock von Sa-Atz zu Sa-Atz
mit hünig sprenkem stimmstummel.
balzerig würmelte es im männechensee
und den weibern ward so pfingstig ums heil
zumahn: wenn ein knie-ender sie hirschelte.[61]

Jandl's work offers itself especially to examining how a poetic text – in contrast to journalism, propaganda, memoirs or historiography – chooses to reproduce reality. To give a social historian's assessment of the extraordinary power of Jandl's text and its remarkable condensation of history, I quote Ernst Hanisch:

> Im Grunde steht der nachgeborene Historiker ratlos vor dem Massengeschehen in den Märztagen des Jahres 1938. Massenpsychologische Theorien helfen gewiß einen Schritt weiter bei der Erklärung: aber sie stoßen rasch an ihre Grenzen. Ich kenne keinen Text, der auf einer halben Druckseite jene kollektive Flucht aus der Realität so präzise einfängt und so vielfältig, ironiegesättigt analysiert wie Ernst Jandls Gedicht.[62]

In other words, here is a case where, in the learned opinion of a historian, a creative writer has used the very special linguistic and formal strategies of that highly concentrated specimen of text called a poem to convey, better than any historian could do, the socio-psychological complexities of a given historic event. But even within the range of styles of the genre of lyrical poetry, Jandl's is utterly different to the other texts quoted elsewhere in this book and calls for a short excursus on the subject of its distinctive style. It is indebted to the linguistic experimentation of Expressionism and Dadaism as well as to the nonsense verse of Christian Morgenstern and Joachim Ringelnatz. It is important, too, to note that, as Jandl indicates in his commentary on his poem in "mein gedicht und sein autor", he had just read James Joyce's *Ulysses*.[63] As in the case of Joyce in the latter episodes of that novel (and even more so in *Finnegan's Wake*), Jandl's method of achieving a multiple stratification of meaning is by forming neologisms in which familiar concepts and semantemes are made to merge with each other, causing semantic polyvalence and a rich associativeness. This method, according to Jörg Drews:

eröffnet [...] dem Verständnis des einzelnen Wortes große Freiheiten bzw. Unsicherheiten, denn die Wortneubildungen, die "Hybridisierungen" und Mehrfachdeterminiertheit vieler der verdichteten Einzelworte legen Assoziationen nahe, über deren Stringenz schwieriger zu entscheiden ist als bei den meisten "konventionellen" Gedichten.[64]

Drews' observation regarding the simultaneous liberation and obfuscation of meaning is borne out in the critical literature dealing with the poem, in that the various readings are sometimes in complete agreement with one another and sometimes widely diverging. A table has been drawn up by Jürgen Koppensteiner showing the proportion of familiar nouns, verbs, adjectives and adverbs in the poem to those invented by Jandl, demonstrating optically that those labelled "bekannt" outnumber those under the rubric "neu".[65] But even the first list of semantemes, though consisting of standard vocabulary, are invested with unusual ramifications by the unorthodox co-text of the neologisms, rendering their interpretability, too, more complex. On the one hand, interpretation on the basis of the reader's subjective associations never quite overcomes the risk of speculativeness, while on the other hand, the very nature of the ambiguity evident in the text places the task of endowing meaning partially into the hands of the reader/interpreter. Moreover, the associative method of exegesis is legitimated by Jandl's own use of this interpretative method as applied to his own poems in his lecture "Voraussetzungen, Beispiele und Ziele einer poetischen Arbeitsweise".[66]

Jandl makes no attempt to reproduce the original surface-text of Hitler's speech as quoted above, but rather presents a linguistic hotchpotch, corresponding aurally, perhaps, to the distortions caused by an echoing amplification through several loudspeakers as well as by the twelve-year-old boy's somatic reception of the word-sequence. But this very garbling of the text has the effect of delving down through the surface-text to expose the group-dynamic of the occasion: the relationship between Hitler and his 200,000 listeners. In other words, Jandl does not treat what was said, but rather the questions of what kind of man it was who said it, to whom and under what circumstances it was said and what effect it had. "Er erfindet eine Sprache", Ulrich Greiner says:

in der die Hysterie der Massen schrill und bedrohlich wiederkehrt. Die Worte und die Bedeutungen überlagern sich, so wie der Nachhall der Hitlerrede von den Mauern der Hofburg verzerrt und seinen wahren Sinn bloßgelegt haben mag.[67]

What is clear from even a peremptory, impressionistic reading of the text is that it constitutes an act of myth-dismantling. Jandl's subtle process of deconstruction begins already in the title by dint of its lack of capital letters: "heldenplatz" with a small "h" scales down the pomp of both the location and its architectonic and sculptural semiotics, and by implication the mightiness of the central figure, who, although never named, is obviously Adolf Hitler himself. To put it differently: "ein held" is less awe-inspiring than "ein Held". Grandeur, like beauty, is in the eye of the beholder, and only those who wanted to see Hitler – or were seduced into seeing him – as the "Redeemer of the Nation" projected their quasi-religious aspirations into this, realistically speaking, rather unimposing human figure. There were many in Vienna that day who saw through The "Emperor's New Clothes" and discovered a Führer with a small "f". The eleven-year-old Rudolfine Haiderer was among the working-class schoolchildren who were marched out onto the streets by their teachers to wave swastikas:

> Ich verstand nicht, wofür sich die Menge begeisterte, warum wir uns freuen und jubeln sollten. Soldaten hatte ich schon öfter gesehen, und der "Führer" erschien mir zwergenhaft unscheinbar.[68]

The eight-year-old half-Jewish boy Otto Schenk wrote down his impressions laconically in a school essay the next day (and was awarded top marks for it):

> Gestern war eine große Parade. Ich ging auf den Ring und kletterte auf einen Mast. Ich sah aber sehr wenig, weil ich spät gekommen war. Es war aber gerade genug.[69]

The vast majority, however, reacted as conveyed in the first stanza and last three lines of Jandl's poem, including many who, only a few days previously, had waved the "Kruckenkreuz" emblem and chanted the "Fatherland Front" slogan "Rot-weiß-rot bis in den Tod!" The nineteen-year-old Viennese Jewish girl Gertrude Scholz was standing on the Heldenplatz incredulously watching the crowd "going wild, ecstatic about their *Führer*", like "the rabbit before the snake".[70] The jubilation of the previous few days, wrote the historian Helmut Andics, reached a crescendo on the Heldenplatz:

> Pressephotographen und Wochenschaureporter belieferten die ganze Welt mit dem Anblick eines Volkes, das vor Begeisterung außer Rand und Band geraten schien. [...] Kein Trommelfell, das nicht zu platzen drohte, wenn das

Chorgeschrei der Tausenden, Zehntausenden, Hundert-
tausenden erklang: "Ein Volk, ein Reich, ein Führer".[71]

The way in which Hitler was received is reproduced in the
first line of Jandl's poem: "der glanze heldenplatz zirka/
versaggerte im maschenhaften männchenmeere". The
ambience is summed up brilliantly in Jandl's amalgamation
of the adjective "ganz" with the noun "Glanz". The latter
component conveys what Minna Lachs above observed about
the grandeur of the *locale*, while "ganz" reminds us of the
vastness of the crowd. And yet the defamiliarizing dadaist use
of a noun ("Glanz") as an inflected adjective with a small "g"
subtly suggests that the glorification is very much tongue-in-
cheek. Historically speaking, many of the apparent multitude
of supporters had to be bussed in from outlying districts.
Also, the impression that the Heldenplatz was completely
thronged with people was, like almost everything to do with
National Socialism, a result of media manipulation. Private
photos of the occasion show that there were quite a few
sparsely populated sections of the square which were
carefully omitted in the photos and film sequences that went
around the world that day.[72] One could see this sobering fact
as being conveyed in the deflating modification "zirka" in the
sense of "the entire, splendid Heldenplatz (approximately
speaking)".[73] On another level, as some commentators have
pointed out, "zirka" is made by its German rather than Latin
spelling to be suggestive of "Zirkus". Peter Pabisch writes:
"Die glanzvolle Show fand in der arenaartigen Anlage des
Wiener Heldenplatzes statt und kam einer Zirkusvorstellung
nahe",[74] and Jörg Drews asks:

> Sollen wir aus "zirka" auch "Zirkus" heraushören? Als
> despektierliche Kennzeichnung der Kundgebung? Weil die
> Menge die rednerischen Bravourleistungen des Führers
> bejubelte wie die Darbietungen eines Zirkuskünstlers?[75]

Both observations are borne out by Carl Zuckmayer's eye-
witness account, quoted above, of the atmosphere of
Fasching celebrations in the days of the Anschluss, but one
could expand on this argument in the context of the hunting
leitmotif which becomes apparent later in the poem: the
"Führer's" hypnotic effect on the masses and their abject self-
subjugation to his will are conjured up by the image of the
trainer of circus-animals who is applauded for whipping the
beasts into disciplined submission and making them perform
acts alien to their nature. The self-prostration of individuals
and their collective transformation into a mindless herd is
corroborated by the reduction in the next word of "Menschen"

to "männchen": this is a sea not of humans but rather of Lilliputians, dwarfed personalities and stunted minds that grovel or sit up and beg ("Männchen machen"). That they are in human terms failures, flops, dupes who become all too readily obliterated as individuals is doubly contained in the proximity of the neologism "versaggerte" to "versagen" (= to be a failure, to break down) and "versacken" (= to sink, cave in, become submerged). Jandl himself aids in the interpretation of "maschenhaft", a distortion of "massenhaft", by introducing the concept of a "Fischfangmotiv".[76] "Maschen" are the mesh of a net and make one think of Peter Pabisch's description of 15 March as the day "als Hitler vom Balkon des Äußeren Wiener Burghofes mit unheilvoll fesselnder Stimme eine lammhaft dumme Menschenmasse in seine Netze lockte".[77] For Jörg Drews the hybrid "maschenhaft" points in the direction of "Maschendraht" (wire-netting). The concentration camps, which already existed in Germany and would soon do so in Austria, are further suggested by "-haft", which, taken as a noun, means "imprisonment". "Masche" is also used colloquially in the sense of "trickery" or "hoax", and as such could serve as an indication of the delusive techniques of mass suggestion applied so expertly by the choreographing of Hitler's meetings.[78]

In this last connotation the word "Masche" links up etymologically with "Maske", which appears in similarly distorted form in the next line:

> drunter auch frauen die ans maskelknie
> zu heften heftig sich versuchten, hoffensdick.

On the subject of Hitler's mask, Erich Fromm's comments are relevant:

> Wenn man Hitlers Persönlichkeit verstehen will, muß man sich klarmachen, daß die Maske, die das wahre Gesicht dieses ruhelos umhergetriebenen Menschen bedeckte, die eines liebenswürdigen, höflichen, beherrschten, fast scheuen Menschen war. Besonders Frauen gegenüber war er höflich, und er hat nie versäumt, ihnen bei passender Gelegenheit Blumen mitzubringen oder zu schicken.[79] [...] Auch abgesehen von den persönlichen und gesellschaftlichen Gründen, die Hitler für diese äußere Tünche gehabt haben mag, war sie auch in anderer Hinsicht von großem Wert für ihn. Half sie ihm doch, die Industriellen, die Militärs und die nationalistischen politischen Führer in Deutschland ebenso wie viele ausländische Politiker hinters Licht zu führen, die sich vielleicht von seiner Brutalität und Gewalttätigkeit abgestoßen gefühlt hätten.[80]

The mask helped him to dupe the masses, too. In Jandl's text the image "Maske" merges with that of a "Muskelknie", evocative of the bare knees of the Hitler Youth and the knee-revealing Lederhosen of their superiors. What Pabisch calls the fetishistic Nazi emphasis of the muscular knee[81] takes on an ironic dimension with reference to Hitler, whose knees were often on show but were anything but muscular. And yet despite his somewhat flaccid physique, his erotic appeal to the opposite sex was undeniable. Luckily, tastes and modes of behaviour change, but it is evident that in those times of thoroughly militarized values and socialization the figure of the dashing ("schneidig") officer and the angular ("zackig") bodily movements of soldiers on parade still had a perverse sex appeal. Carl Zuckmayer relates an incident from 13 March:

> Ich wollte mir Zigarren kaufen, aber die Tabaktrafikantin, die mich jahrelang bedient hatte, eine fünfzigjährige Witwe, rannte hinter ein paar deutschen Soldaten her, um ihnen Zigaretten in die Tasche zu stecken. "Daitsche Brieder", kreischte sie und verdrehte die Augen ekstatisch. Der Schaum schien ihr vorm Mund zu stehn. Sie soll sich, als die erste deutsche Einheit einrückte, auf die Straße gekniet haben.[82]

Also in the case of Hitler, his reputed "Nasenwurzelblick", that is, his trick of fixing his steely blue eyes on the nose bridge of his opposite number, as well as the way he screamed himself hoarse during speeches, caused men to tremble at his glance and thrill to his words (even when they misheard them) and women to swoon in his proximity. As the Nazi "Heimatdichter" Hans Kloepfer enthused in his fawning "Steirischer Bergbauerngruß" of spring 1939:

> Der schaut dir in d'Augn
> und druckt dir die Hond,
> und woaß, ehst no redtst,
> wo's di klemmt umanond.[83]

Ernst Hanisch quotes a former member of the National Socialist "Bund Deutscher Mädel" who recalled the "Hitler experience" fifty years later:

> Man hat dem Führer in die Augen geschaut, in diese stahlblauen Augen, und es ist einfach durch und durch gegangen. Ich werde das mein Leben lang nicht vergessen ...[84]

At his mass meetings, supposedly mature men and women reacted as hysterically as teenagers do today at pop concerts. Minna Lachs tells of an encounter with an old woman coming from Heldenplatz:

> "Wissen S'", sprach sie mich vertraulich an, "ich hab' weggehen müssen, weil mir die Füß' vom langen Stehen so weh getan haben. Aber ich hab' ihn gesehn, unseren Führer. Jetzt kann ich ruhig sterben". Sie wischte sich die Augen.[85]

Franz Werfel attempted to recreate the frenzied atmosphere of the days leading up to Hitler's speech by describing the public behaviour in front of the huge Hitler portrait in the German Tourist Office in the Kärntnerstraße:

> Das Seltsame aber war, daß nicht nur die Jugend und die hysterischen Weiber sich in der Blutwolke des Massenrausches wanden. Ich sah Männer meinesgleichen, ältere und alte, den Siegern keineswegs zugehörig, die derwischhafte Laute ausstießen und mit den Armen schlugen, als seien das gestutzte Flügel. [...] Vor jenem Reisebüro hatte die hin und her wogende Menge ein religiöses Schweigen befallen. Irgend jemand hielt eine Rede in langen schwülen Lauten, wie ein besessener Schamane. Weiber fielen plötzlich aufs Knie, streckten die Arme zum Himmel und beteten den Drachen an. Neben mir ein altes Mütterchen, das wahrscheinlich gar nicht wußte, was vorging, brach in schüttelndes Schluchzen aus.[86]

The stale phrase "hysterische Weiber" was in Werfel's misogynous times all too easily bandied about to explain the cultural decline which was felt by so many intellectuals to be taking place already before the First World War. But as Werfel points out, women made up only a part of the general hysteria in Vienna in those days.

Jandl introduces the description of female behaviour on Heldenplatz with the word "drunter". This can mean "*among* the men ('männchenmeere') there were also women who behaved insanely". But "drunter" can also mean "*beneath* the men", which would reflect the strictly androcentric and hierarchical nature of fascism. Nazism was a thoroughly male phenomenon, even if it could not have functioned without the aid of those millions of women who had completely internalized its phallocratic ideology. This, in a sense, is what Jandl's poem is about. Friedrich Torberg in *Auch das war Wien* used sexual imagery to characterize the self-prostration of a large majority of the population of Vienna, male and female, at the moment of the city's penetration by German tank convoys and bomber planes:

> Ach, und das Fremde in ihr [= der Stadt Wien], die vielen
> fremden Soldaten, die vielen fremden Autos und fremde
> Polizisten sogar – dem allen müßte sie doch, wenn es die
> Stadt noch wäre, desto unverkennbarer sich entgegenheben,
> desto beharrlicher widerstehen, stumm und starr und
> steinern. Aber sie widersteht nicht. Sie gibt nach. Sie gibt sich
> preis und gibt sich hin. [...] es [das Fremde] war eingedrungen
> in die Stadt und die Stadt nahm es auf, schmiegsam und
> willfährig, und versank darin, und war eine andere Stadt.[87]

George Clare used the same coital metaphor to describe the
frenetic abandon of the Viennese of both sexes:

> The whole city behaved like an aroused woman, vibrating,
> writhing, moaning and sighing lustfully for orgasm and
> release. This is not purple writing. It is an exact description of
> what Vienna was and felt like on Monday, 14 March 1938, as
> Hitler entered her.[88]

In Jandl's poem the women try ardently ("heftig") to cling to
the Führer's knee – or rather seduce *themselves* into doing so
("*sich* versuchten"). The reflexive pronoun, which belongs to
the verb "heften", is displaced in such a way as to suggest
that it is coupled with "versuchten" instead, changing the
intransitive verb "to try" into the transitive verb "to tempt" or
"seduce" and making it unconventionally reflexive. The verb
thus takes on the connotation of complicity, of people
willingly succumbing to the seduction. In that tiny word
"sich" is contained a refutation of the popular Austrian
presentation of the Anschluss as a German assault
("Überfall"), and of Hitler himself as a diabolical seducer of
innocent people. In other words, it suggests that a readiness
on the part of the supposed "victims" was necessary to effect
an annexation as smoothly running and enthusiastically
applauded as was the Anschluss.

The impression of carnality is intensified in "hoffensdick", the
formulation being much more physical than the somewhat
elevated concept "zukunftsschwanger" which it parodies in
that it conveys the very bloatedness of pregnancy. The idea of
impregnation is expanded to that of bestiality in the next line:
"und brüllzten wesentlich". The tension between the two last
words echoes that dichotomy which characterized the Nazi
Period in general: that between humanity and animality. In
his own commentary Jandl assigns "brüllzten" to the animal
sphere, while "wesentlich" is meant "als menschliche Marke"
to indicate that we are dealing with human beings.[89] Not only
do humans foresake their inherent rationality when they
bellow ("brüllen"), but the act is made more animal and lewd
by the insertion of a sibilant into the past tense form and by

thus blending the word "brüllen" with "brunsten", which means male animals' rutting as well as female animals' being on heat. One could read "brüllzen" also as a collage of "brüllen" with "balzen", which means the courtship display of birds. The interaction between the "Führer" and the masses on the Heldenplatz is registered as a "Brunstschrei", a mutual mating call, and, by extension, the Austrian Anschluss as the mating season between the German stag and the Austrian hind. The hunting motif will return in the third stanza to strengthen this conceit.

In the second stanza and first three lines of the last stanza the text focuses on Hitler himself:

> verwogener stirnscheitelunterschwang
> nach nöten nördlich, kechelte
> mit zu-nummernder aufs bluten feilzer stimme
> hinsensend sämmertliche eigenwäscher.

First his appearance: the adjective "verwegen" (daring, bold) would correspond to the picture that Hitler wished to project of himself, but here its claim to truth is undermined in one breath by being crossed with "verlogen" (mendacious, false). The neologism "stirnscheitelunterschwang" is, by its very length, a parody of the elongated compounds and sterile jargon of which Nazi rhetoric was so fond. When spoken in the jagged way of Ernst Jandl's own recording of the poem, the word reminds us of Charlie Chaplin's sonal and facial mimicry of Hitler in *The Great Dictator*. In a very condensed way the word evokes Hitler's physiognomy and body language: the hair parting ("-scheitel-"), the wad of hair that constantly fell down ("-unter-") over his forehead ("stirn-") and was swung ("-schwang") or stroked back into place at highpoints of his speeches. Furthermore, the collage "-unter-schwang" combines "Überschwang" (= exuberance, rapture) with a technical term from gymnastics, "Unterschwung", which suggests the machine-like acrobatics of taut bodies, reminding us of the Nazi cult of "der gestählte Körper" and its origins in the romantic, athletic and anti-Semitic nationalism of Turnvater Jahn.

And yet, as in Chaplin's caricature, Hitler himself was at best "nach nöten nördlich", if we interpret this phrase as meaning "zur Not nordisch". One of the more comical anomalies of the Hitler Period and its ideology of Aryan purity was how far its own leaders – with the exception of Heydrich – fell short of fulfilling the propagated biological ideal. Since Jandl's wordplay not only permits but demands a second, third and fourth interpretation of each text particle, it is legitimate to read "nach nöten nördlich" complementarily as a biographical note on the young Austrian Hitler: after the second rejection of his application to study painting at the Academy of Fine Arts in Vienna, Hitler lived in various hostels for the homeless and scraped a living from selling his own handmade postcards of vistas of Vienna. To escape the Austrian draft he went to Munich, where he settled and, in the course of time, reinvented himself as German. In this way "nach nöten nördlich" could be interpreted also as meaning: "nach den Nöten, die Hitler in Wien erlebte, ging er dorthin, wo er sich mit dem weiter nördlich befindlichen, 'echteren' Deutschtum identifizierte". And/or: since he could not achieve the respect of others in Vienna, it was necessary ("vonnöten") to go North, and/or to adhere to the already established theory of Nordic racial supremacy in order to gain self-respect.

The way the "Führer" spoke is described with the neologism "kechelte", a conflation of "keuchen" (to wheeze, gasp for breath) and "hecheln" (to pant quickly like a dog), and conveys how towards the end of outbursts of stridency his voice often became scratchy and choking. This process, according to the poem, occurred "mit zu-nummernder aufs bluten feilzer stimme". The first adjective is a bastardization of "zunehmend", an adverb which describes the well-known rhetorical strategy, by no means invented but certainly exploited to the full by Hitler, of starting with quiet and paced, almost intimate speech and advancing, sometimes abruptly, to a crescendo of shrieking. But why is the idea of numbers introduced? Jörg Drews suggests that the raucous screaming has the mass effect of transforming individuals into digits.[90] "'zu-nummernder'", writes Peter Pabisch, "mag das Phänomen der 'Nummer' herausstreichen, zu der jeder Mensch in der Diktatur degradiert wird".[91] This metaphorical use of number brings one upon the idea of its more concrete and sinister realization in the form of the tattooed numbers on the arms of concentration camp inmates.

The trope of blood in the next adjectival phrase has, needless to say, a long German history, from Bismarck's martial and authoritarian state that set about achieving hegemony over continental Europe by "Blut und Eisen" to the Nazi ideology combining "Aryan" blood with territory and roots in the geogenic slogan "Blut und Boden". The fact that the word "bluten" is preceded by the preposition "aufs" gives it an added dimension of personal aggression by echoing the common usages "bis aufs Blut hassen" or "bis aufs Blut bekämpfen" – a fight to the death against "sämmertliche eigenwäscher". The noun derives from "Eigenbrödler" and means in Jandl's own analysis "individualists",[92] while the adjective is a fusion of "sämtlich" and "jämmerlich", as all those who resisted total "Gleichschaltung" were seen from the Nazi perspective as miserable wretches. The gerund "hinsensend" evokes the image of the Hitler figure cutting down "eigenwäscher" with a scythe. Here the medieval topos of the "Sensenmann" or "Death the Reaper" is being drawn upon – fittingly, when one considers the amount of dissidents who met their death under the Nazi regime, but also in respect to Hitler's own personality and what Erich Fromm called his "necrophilic character",[93] which only seven years later would culminate in his calling down death and destruction upon the entire German people for having disappointed him. The coinage "feilzer" in relation to Hitler's voice suggests that it has the grating sound of filing. The word is also close to "falsch", and furthermore conjures up the meretriciousness of Hitler's system of values by its association with "feil", meaning venal, and "feilschen", meaning to haggle over a ware with the object of buying it for a low price or selling it for a high one. One could make this fit the occasion by seeing the Heldenplatz propaganda display as a kind of gigantic promotion show to sell an idea which only a few days previously the majority of citizens had opposed: the self-dissolution of the state of Austria.

The last stanza is introduced by a line with a single word that brings the hunting conceit into play once more:

> pirsch!
> döppelte der gottelbock von Sa-Atz zu Sa-Atz
> mit hünig sprenkem stimmstummel.

"Auf Pirsch gehen" describes the act of stalking the deer and taking up position from which to shoot it. In Jandl's own recitation of the text, he makes "pirsch!" sound like a shot. Whereas above I suggested that in the first stanza the Hitler figure could be construed as a stag mating with the hind (= the masses), here he is the huntsman. It must be remembered that the whole sphere of stag-hunting played, and in some areas still plays, a very central role in the myth of the Austrian and Bavarian male. The Austrian "Weidmann" was the equivalent of the Spanish bull-fighter, the Alpine he-man *par excellence*, stalwart hero of so many "Heimatfilme" and drawing-room paintings, the member of a daring elite with their own costume, jargon, rituals and ethos, who ventured out in isolation, with rifle and binoculars, into the magnificence of the wooded and craggy mountains to seek the moment of truth with the noble stag, and then proudly decorate the walls of their "gute Stube" with antlers, the mark and fetish of masculinity, as trophies of the hunters' prowess and power. It was one of Göring's favourite leisure-time roles, and Hitler, too, was wont to pose for photographic portraits in an outfit and against a backdrop that quoted from this androcentric world.

The verb "döppelte" could be linked up with the motifs of mask, hoax and venality by its being reminiscent of the word "doppelzüngig" (devious, duplicitous) or "doppelgesichtig" (two-faced), or in characterizing a person who plays a "Doppelspiel" (double game) or speaks "doppeldeutig" (ambiguously). The "Führer", indeed, is a "gottelbock", playing a double role, on the one hand as a god (albeit a reduced one as a result of the lower-case initial letter "g" as well as the diminutive "-el"), and on the other as a stag ("Hirschbock"), ruttish buck, satyr, Priapus – a false idol of lust. "gottel-" is also close to "Gockel", which means in human terms a poseur, a peacock. Jörg Drews extracts from these lines the deflating image of "Doppelbock",[94] a reference to the heady beer favoured at Nazi beerhall meetings, and by extension, the intoxicating effect of such occasions. Hitler springs "von Sa-Atz zu Sa-Atz", the bisecting of the word "Satz" not only replicating Hitler's staccato articulation (the "stimmstummel" of the next line) when he became excited, but also exposing the threat behind the sentences and the force behind the "Führer": the SA, his dreaded Storm Troopers. Moreover, it brings to the surface an image that would otherwise lie submerged in the word "Satz": that of "Atzung", a term from the hunting world meaning fodder laid out for game, or on a metaphorical level in this particular context, feeding the mob with what it is prepared to swallow.

The "Führer" now speaks or rather shrieks – as the capitals in the words "von Sa-Atz zu Sa-Atz", the only ones in the entire text, indicate – "mit hünig sprenkem stimmstummel", with truncated exclamations that blast or gallop forth ("sprengen") in a manner supposedly evocative of ancient German gods and heroes ("Hünen"). Drews sees in "sprenkem" a montage of "sich spreizen" and "streng",[95] which would correspond to the contradictions in Hitler's behaviour as delineated above: on the one hand putting on airs, splaying one's feathers like a peacock, and on the other, harsh, severe, rigid. The effect is the precalculated one:

balzerig würmelte es im männechensee
und den weibern ward so pfingstig ums heil
zumahn: wenn ein knie-ender sie hirschelte.

As throughout the whole poem there is a dense mixing of metaphors here too. In other words, what is considered by normative aesthetics to be a rhetorical error is here made into a stylistic device. The metaphors are once more drawn from the spheres of fishing, hunting and mating. The "männechensee", the lake teeming with mannikins waiting to be netted, respond to the peacock's courtship display ("balzerig"). The verb "wimmeln" is crossed with the noun "Wurm", changing the verb from "teeming" to convey the image of "wriggling". In the verb, one could say, "ist ein Wurm drin" ("there is something fishy"). The people are not only reduced in stature to dwarfs but transform themselves into worms asking to be trampled upon.

The penultimate line touches upon probably the most grotesque feature of Nazism: its secularized religiosity. It draws on vocabulary from the Christian tradition: the more antiquated form of "wurde" ("ward") strikes a biblical note, while "pfingstig ums heil" recalls the Pentecost, the Holy Ghost's descension in the form of tongues of fire to implant the new message of salvation ("*Heil*sbotschaft") in Christ's disciples. Jandl himself explains the use of "pfingstig" simply as a means of indicating the time of year.[96] But there is surely much more to it than that. Firstly, Whit was yet a long way off from the occasion of the Heldenplatz speech. Secondly, it was common for Nazi leaders, lackeys, journalists and poets to plunder the rhetoric of Christian mysticism in order to find superlatives of adoration for their "Führer", including the phrase "Pfingstwunder", by which they meant less the time of year than the miracle of Hitler's "tongue of fire". Even in the much used "Heil!" there was an overtone of "Heiland" (Redeemer). Victor Klemperer, writing on the phenomenon of Hitler's "Selbstvergottung und stilistische Selbstangleichung an den Christus des Neuen Testaments",[97] gives some examples of the systematic apotheosization of the "gottelbock" before and after 15 March:

Im Juli 1934 sagte Göring in einer Rede vor dem Berliner Rathaus: "Wir sind alle, vom einfachen SA-Mann bis zum Ministerpräsidenten, sind von Adolf Hitler und durch Adolf Hitler". In den Wahlaufrufen des Jahres 1938 zur Bestätigung des Österreichsanschlusses, zur Billigung Großdeutschlands heißt es, Hitler sei "das Werkzeug der Vorsehung", und dann im alttestamentarischen Stil: "die Hand muß verdorren, die Nein schreibt". Baldur von Schirach bestimmt die

Geburtsstadt des Führers, Braunau, zum "Wallfahrtsort der deutschen Jugend". Baldur von Schirach gibt auch "Das Lied der Getreuen" heraus, "Verse ungenannter österreichischer Hitlerjugend aus den Jahren der Verfolgung 1933 bis 1937"; darin heißt es: "... Es gibt so viele, die dir nie begegnen, und denen du trotzdem der Heiland bist".[98]

The Organization Book of the NSDAP (National Socialist German Workers' Party), distributed in 1938, contains the Twelve Commandments for National Socialists, the first and foremost appropriating and adapting the first Mosaic Commandment as well as the Catholic doctrine of Papal Infallibility: "Der Führer hat immer recht!" The *Klagenfurter Zeitung*, reporting on the Heldenplatz speech, shamelessly used the concepts "Gospel" and "Resurrection" in a tone that is both cliché-ridden and tastelessly devotional:

> Über Nacht ist die Stadt eine andere geworden. Das gedrückte Leben ist aus ihr gewichen, die verschiedenen Aufmärsche sind verschwunden, *eine* Parole beherrscht alle Menschen: "Heil dem Führer, Sieg und Heil dem gesamten Deutschen Reich!"

> Die Evangelien deutschen Lebens, zu gleicher Zeit in allen Städten und Dörfern Österreichs ausgerufen, formen sich zu immer größeren, ergreifenden Jubelchören.[99] [....]

> Diese Stunden, jene der Unterdrückung und jene der Auferstehung, sie werden Gebete bleiben, wenn selbst von den Stammelnden der tiefsten Ergriffenheit das Lallen ihres jubelnden Mundes verklungen sein wird.[100]

On 9 April, the "Tag des Großdeutschen Reiches", the Nazi Lord Mayor of Vienna, Hermann Neubauer, surpassed himself with his words of homage to Hitler: "Allmächtiger, wir danken Dir! Führer, führe uns! Deutschland, nimm uns an Dein heiliges Herz!"[101] And the Catholic priest Fr Ottokar Kernstock conferred upon this revolting concoction of fascism and Christian mysticism a kind of sacerdotal *imprimatur* with his poem, sold in postcard form in all the newsagents of Vienna:

> Das Hakenkreuz im weißen Feld
> Auf feuerrotem Grunde
> Hat uns mit stolzem Mut beseelt,
> Es schlägt in unsrer Runde

> Kein Herz, das feig
> Die Treue bricht.
> Wir fürchten Tod und Teufel nicht:
> Mit uns ist Gott im Bunde![102]

But the Protestant Church was not to be outdone in tastelessness. In a hymn written in 1939 in celebration of Hitler's birthday, he is likened to the Christ Child, while the depiction of his mother seems strangely indebted to the Catholic cult of Mary:

> Führer von Gottes Gnaden erkoren,
> Retter des deutschen Volkes zu sein!
> Selig die Mutter, die dich geboren!
> Dank noch in ihren Hügel hinein!
> Als du hilflos im Arm ihr gelegen,
> als sie dich drückte an ihre Brust,
> hat sie von deinen irdischen Wegen
> in die Unsterblichkeit nichts gewußt! ...

After this mawkish overture, the "Male Principle" has somehow to be re-established while preserving the otherworldly aura:

> Und es schüttete Gott seine Gaben
> hernieder auf des Erwählten Haupt;
> und er stählte zum Manne den Knaben,
> zum Manne, an den ganz Deutschland glaubt!
> Und es reißt in heimlicher Stille
> Wunder um Wunder ans Licht, daß sich
> des Volkes Wiedergeburt erfülle,
> Größter der Deutschen, Führer durch dich![103]

Also the Baroque tradition of erotic mysticism was plundered in the panegyrics written in honour of Hitler by third-rate poetasters. In Hans Kloepfer's eulogy "Dem Führer", Hitler, in a heady concoction of highly disparate images, is not only presented in the first stanza as an ineffable and almighty Being with the thundering voice of God's Last Judgement, but in the second one as a copious inseminator of the receptive womb of the fructuous Germanic Mother Earth:

> Und ob ich dich von hundert Bildern schaute,
> ich fasse Deines Wesens Allmacht nicht,
> wenn Deine Stimme, die uns liebvertraute,
> den Feinden tönt wie Gottes Weltgericht.
>
> Des Ahnenkeimgrunds tiefe Lebensquellen,
> geklärt in früher Fron und eigner Zucht,
> ließ deine Kraft zum Segensstrome schwellen
> für deutschen Erdreichs überreiche Frucht.[104]

As Ulrich Weinzierl writes:

> Beinahe als Markenzeichen solcher Art von Poesie konnte das unübersehbar pseudosakrale, bisweilen auch erotisch gefärbte Vokabular gelten: Immer war da von Segen und

Gebet, von Vereinigung und Erlösung und vom "heiligen Reich" die gebundene Rede. Gerade die für die massenhysterische Atmosphäre charakeristische Mischung aus Brunst und Inbrunst hat auch Ernst Jandl in seinem lautmalenden, Buchstaben versetzenden Gedicht "wien: heldenplatz" wiedergegeben.[105]

To judge from the syntax of the last two lines of Jandl's poem, which as elsewhere in the text is conventional, the neologism "zumahn" makes sense as "zumute", yielding more or less the following meaning: "the women felt so pentecostal about salvation (by the "Führer")", or as "zumal", meaning: "the women became so pentecostal about salvation, especially since ..." But this word, too, is contaminated. Pabisch offers the explanation that "zumahn" sounds like "zumal", but that the root syllable "-mahn" is connected with "Mahnung" and "Mahnmal" and the fatal consequences of this hunting scene.[106] The women became ecstatic "wenn ein knie-ender sie hirschelte". The concluding verb not only sounds like "herrschen" (= to dominate) but also brings us back to the mating theme, as does the bisection of "knieender", linking the knee-displaying "Führer" with the "Zwölfender" of hunting jargon: the royal stag with twelve points on its antlers, "der röhrende Hirsch", as depicted in so many petit-bourgeois bedrooms. In Jandl's highly charged overlaying of the pseudo-sacral with the obscene, of "Inbrunst" with "Brunst" – and what technique could more fittingly characterize Nazism? – one can hear the Heldenplatz reverberating to the throaty bell of the rutting stag answered by the mesmerized and supine chanting of "Ein Volk, ein Reich, ein Führer", in the words of Manès Sperber, "wie Schreie eines wollüstigen Leidens".[107]

That very evening, after being worked up by Hitler's speech, the Viennese, known for their "golden heart", were to become the veritable manhunters. In the depiction by Friedrich Torberg:

Hämisch grinsten und lauerten sie, lüstern dämpfte ihnen der Atem aus schiefem Maul, prüfenden Blicks umfaßten sie das Revier ihrer Beute, in gierigem Auslug, in sprungbereiter Witterung [...].[108]

Manès Sperber also made use of the hunting metaphor to depict the lot of Europe's Jews, which on that day, 15 March, 1938, was to enter its worst phase in Austria:

Sie hatten noch den Ausdruck von Willen in den Gesichtern,
die Gebärden tätiger Menschen, aber sie waren gehetztes
Wild. Der Kreis der Treiber und der Jäger schloß sich immer
enger um sie, und sie vergaßen es keinen Augenblick.[109]

Ernst Hanisch summarizes the thrust of Jandl's poem thus:

Jene ichschwachen Individuen, die im "männchenmeer" sich
stark und überlegen fühlen; die sexuellen Vibrationen einer
kollektiven Erregung; die Erwartungen auf ein besseres Leben
nach dem "Anschluß" – "hoffensdick", scheinschwanger, und
nach einigen Monaten ist der Bauch leer, die Hoffnung weg;
der charismatische Führer "verwogener stirnscheitelunterschwang", mit seiner "aufs bluten feilzer stimme", aufs
Töten ausgerichtet, den individuellen Widerstand
("eigenwäscher") gegen die postulierte Volksgemeinschaft
"hinsensend"; der Nationalsozialismus als politische Religion,
im Zentrum der Verehrung der "gottelbock" stehend: der Tanz
um das Animalische, die Rasse, der Bock als Gott; die uralten
Männlichkeits- und Weiblichkeitsrituale, der Mann als Jäger,
als Krieger, als sexuell Potenter; die Frauen empfängnisbereit,
gierig nach dem "maskelknie", damit ihnen "pfingstig ums
heil" werde.[110]

3. The aftermath

The Jews of Vienna, who made up 9.4% of the city's population, had felt secure and very much at home until the Anschluss, despite the anti-Semitic manifestations of Austro-fascism. "Es lebte sich gut und heiter in Wien", wrote Elisabeth Castonier, "in dieser einmaligen beschwingten Atmosphäre, die nichts völlig ernst nehmen wollte".[111] In her autobiographical novel *Eine Österreicherin erlebt den Anschluß*, Lili Körber quotes a Viennese publisher named Dr Loewy as follows in a diary entry dated 1 March:

> Heute behauptet Dr Loewy nicht mehr, daß eine Gleichschaltung Österreichs unmöglich sei, er meint nur, es werde einige Zeit dauern und auch nicht in so brutaler Weise durchgeführt werden wie im Reich. "Vergessen Sie nicht: auch unsere Nazi sind noch Österreicher, also kulanter, menschlicher".[112]

The then medical student Hans Schauder reminisced many years later on the deludedness of the Viennese Jews ensconced in their leisurely, urbane and congenial coffee-house culture:

> Im Kaffeehaus fühlte ich mich als ein glücklicher Wiener, respektiert und völlig integriert in die Stadt. Es wäre mir nicht im Traum eingefallen, daß sie mich je würde hinausjagen können. Hier war nur Freundlichkeit, Menschlichkeit. Hinterher habe ich begriffen, daß auch das zur Wiener Illusion gehört hat. Die Juden haben alle, solange es nur irgend ging, am Kaffeehausbesuch festgehalten. Sie haben sich an diese Illusion geklammert und nicht gewußt, daß ihre Mörder schon um sie herum gesessen sind. Es gibt eine Geschichte: Da sitzen zwei Juden im Kaffeehaus. Der eine sagt: "Wissen Sie schon, Blau hat sich umgebracht". Der andere antwortet: "Pst, da sitzt er. Er weiß es noch nicht". Auch wir wußten es noch nicht ...[113]

Robert Breuer quotes a comment he heard in the journalist café Rebhuhn on Sunday, 13 March, which, like Dr Loewy's remarks, typified the Jewish impression of their fellow-citizens:

> "Es wird schon nicht so arg werden wie in Deutschland", sagten sie, "die österreichische Mentalität ist doch so anders als die preußische, und die alte Wiener Gemütlichkeit läßt sich nicht wie schmutziges Badewasser ausschütten!"[114]

What in fact came to pass exceeded all expectations by far. On 11 March, the theatre director Rudolf Beer had spoken optimistically in the company of the cultural historian Egon Friedell: "Verwienerte Nazis – die werden nie grausam sein",[115] only to be beaten half to death by those very same "verwienerte Nazis" some days later. Both he and Friedell committed suicide in the face of the upsurge of intense racism.

One writer after another describes the shock of seeing former acquaintances known to them as antifascists suddenly reappear in the new role of Nazi sympathizer. The Viennese cabaret artist Gerhard Bronner wrote:

> Einige Wochen nach dem Einmarsch der deutschen Truppen und der Auslöschung Österreichs traf ich einen meiner Freunde, einen, der gemeinsam mit mir gegen Hitler demonstriert hatte, wieder. Er trug die Uniform der Hitler-Jugend und wollte grußlos an mir vorbeigehen. Ich stellte ihn: "Sag einmal, wieso bist du bei der Ha-Jot?" "Man muß mit dem Zeitgeist gehen", sagte er herablassend. "Es hat sich viel verändert in diesen Tagen – oder ist dir das nicht aufgefallen?" "Schon", erwiderte ich schüchtern, "aber du hast doch noch vor ein paar Wochen mit mir gemeinsam gegen Hitler demonstriert" ... Mein ehemaliger "Mitstreiter" war überhaupt nicht peinlich berührt. Er sah mir gelassen ins Auge und sagte: "Noch so eine Verleumdung, und ich hau' dir die Goschen ein".[116]

Adi Wimmer was told of a very similar experience of mind-boggling apostasy by the prominent Klagenfurt surgeon Dr Georg Lexer. He and a close friend had been distributing anti-Hitler leaflets as late as 13 March:

> A few days after Austria's demise Lexer was thunderstruck when he saw his pal once again distributing leaflets, *Nazi* leaflets this time. "How can you," he confronted him, "campaign for the Nazis when only last week we two campaigned against them?" The friend fixed him with cold eyes. "If you repeat that lie ever again, you *Saujud*, I'll kick your teeth in".[117]

Erwin Hartl claims that in stereotyping Vienna as the "Metropole der Gemütlichkeit", people overlooked the "stets grassierende Stimmungs-Labilität" of its citizens: "Das sprichwörtlich Goldene Herz berauschte sich immer gern an Extremen. Echte Nächstenliebe konnte vehement umschlagen in puren Nächstenhaß".[118] Edward Arie, an employee of the commercial firm Bunzl & Biach in Vienna, went to work on Monday, 14 March after a two-week long business trip:

My colleagues were suddenly totally changed – for the most part they were no longer the people who had been my friends a few weeks earlier and with whom I'd go out for lunch. They suddenly behaved with reserve, not to say hostility. A few of them showed their rejection of me quite clearly and openly. There were very few who wished to show me that nothing had changed.[119]

When he was arrested along with the 12 other Jews in the firm on 10 November, 1938, and taken away on an open truck, the rest of the staff cheered.

Manès Sperber made a more realistic estimation of the situation than most of his fellow-Jews:

Auch das gehörte zur widerspruchsvollsten Logik meines Lebens: ich liebte eine Stadt, deren Bewohner sich singend und grölend ihres goldenen Herzens rühmten und zugleich auf ihren hemmungslosen Judenhaß stolz waren. Es war vorauszusehen, daß die Nazis da leichter als in irgendeiner deutschen Stadt zahllose eifrige Komplizen finden würden, um Juden zu erniedrigen, und niederträchtige Schergen für die Konzentrationslager und später für die Vernichtungslager.[120]

3.1 The Churches

In the initial stages of the Anschluss the Churches played a prominent role in helping to cement National Socialist power in Austria. On the evening of 15 March, Cardinal Innitzer, though spat upon by anticlerical Nazis while making his way towards the Hotel Imperial to visit the "Führer", told Hitler of his "Freude über die Vereinigung Deutschösterreichs mit dem Reiche" and expressed the determination of Austria's Catholics "tatkräftig am deutschen Aufbauwerk mitzuarbeiten".[121] Six days later, the Austrian bishops issued a pastoral exhorting Catholics to vote for "reunification" in the plebiscite planned for 10 April, although the Bishop of Graz had just spent 24 hours in jail and the Archbishop of Salzburg 48 hours under house arrest. On 22 March they published a "solemn declaration" praising the National Socialists for having repulsed "die Gefahr des alles zerstörenden, gottlosen Bolschewismus".[122] The Bishop of the so-called Old Catholics, a splinter group that did not subscribe to papal infallibility, sent a telegram of welcome to Hitler on 14 March:

> Mit jubelnder Freude begrüßt die Altkatholische Kirche
> Altösterreichs den Retter der Heimat, den großen Führer
> Adolf Hitler, und gelobt ihm Treue für immerdar.[123]

The next day he ordered that masses of thanksgiving be celebrated in all churches on the following Sunday "für die Befreiung der Heimat durch unseren Führer Adolf Hitler" and that from then on a prayer for the "Führer" was to be included in all services.[124] The Protestant Church, which had suffered some discrimination under the *Vaterländische Front* and felt strong affiliations to Prussia, was particularly effusive. Instead of showing solidarity with that other outsider group, the Jewish community, their Church Assembly issued the following address to Hitler in a pastoral on 17 March:

> Im Namen der mehr als 330.000 Evangelischen Deutschen in
> Österreich begrüße ich Sie auf österreichischem Boden. Nach
> einer Unterdrückung, die die schrecklichsten Zeiten der
> Gegenreformation wiederaufleben ließ, kommen Sie als Retter
> aus 5jähriger schwerster Not aller Deutschen hier ohne
> Unterschied des Glaubens.
>
> Gott segne Ihren Weg durch dieses Deutsche Land, und
> unsere Heimat![125]

On 28 March a directive to vote for the Anschluss was read from all the pulpits, accompanied by a note from the President of the new Church Assembly, Robert Kauer, to the effect that Hitler was a leader who taught how love for one's neighbour could be put into practice.[126]

3.2 The persecution begins

No mention was made by any Church of Austria's 185,000 Jews, although the manifestations of ecclesiastical sycophancy described above occurred *after* the public maltreatment of Viennese Jews had begun. Even while Cardinal Innitzer was paying homage to Hitler in the Hotel Imperial on 15 March, the "hunt" referred to metaphorically in Jandl's poem had begun in earnest. To quote Helmut Andics:

> Eine Unterwelt, die hinter der Fassade biederer Bürgerlichkeit
> latent auf die Chance zum einträglichen Fischzug wartete,

mobilisierte sich im März 1938 vor allem in Wien zur Plünderung.

[...] Während begeisterte Illegale nächtelang vor dem Hotel Imperial in der eisigen Märzkälte dem Augenblick entgegenzitterten, in dem sie ihrem Führer zujubeln konnten, gingen die Konjunkturritter mit der Holzhacke auf die Wohnungstüren ihrer jüdischen Nachbarn los. Während die alten Kämpfer nimmermüde treppauf und treppab liefen, um Propagandamaterial für die Volksabstimmung zu verteilen, belagerten biedere Zeitgenossen, die ihr unpolitisches Herz plötzlich für Hitler entdeckt hatten, die improvisierten Gau-, Kreis- und Ortsgruppenleitungen, um irgendeinen Wisch zu ergattern, der sie zur Übernahme dieses oder jenes jüdischen Geschäftes ermächtigte.

[...] Der sogenannte "innere Schweinehund" – um ein mit der Besetzung importiertes Wort zu gebrauchen – feierte fröhliche Urständ. Man kühlte sein Mütchen an der Konkurrenz und füllte sich dabei auch noch die Taschen. Und wo man nicht nach der Brieftasche griff, dort griff man nach dem Menschen. Juden wurden aus den Häusern geschleppt, auf der Straße zusammengetrieben, mit Tafeln behängt, mit Wasserkübeln ausgerüstet und zum allgemeinen Gaudium dazu gezwungen, die letzten noch übriggebliebenen Parolen von Schuschniggs Volksabstimmung von Gehsteigen und Plakatwänden zu entfernen.[127]

On 15 March, two decrees were issued banning Jews from the civil service and withdrawing their right to vote. Also on that day, Jews of all ages and positions, men, women and children, were being rounded up and compelled to scrub off the "vaterländisch" slogans and cramponees that had been painted onto pavements, road surfaces and house walls five days previously. They were forced to go down on their hands and knees and use toothbrushes to make the task more strenuous and humiliating. Jewish women were told to put on their best clothes, make-up and perfume before having to scrub the pavements. SA members painted the slogans anew during the night so as to be able to continue this vicious game for weeks and months. G.E.R. Geyde described one such scene:

Die erste Reibpartie sah ich auf dem Praterstern. Sie mußte das Bild Schuschniggs entfernen, das mit einer Schablone auf dem Sockel eines Monuments gemalt worden war. SA-Leute schleppten einen bejahrten jüdischen Arbeiter und seine Frau durch die beifallklatschende Menge. Tränen rollten der alten Frau über die Wangen, und während sie starr vor sich hinsah und förmlich durch ihre Peiniger hindurchblickte, konnte ich sehen, wie der alte Mann, dessen Arm sie hielt, versuchte,

ihre Hand zu streicheln. "Arbeit für die Juden, endlich Arbeit
für die Juden!" heulte die Menge. "Wir danken unserem
Führer, er hat Arbeit für die Juden beschafft!"[128]

Ulrich Becher and Peter Preses, both of whom had to flee
Vienna in 1938, present the humiliations suffered and the
glee of the Viennese onlookers during the "Aufreibaktionen"
in Act I, Scene II of their play *Der Bockerer*, written in New
York in 1946. It demonstrates, too, how abruptly and
completely the young Nazi movement, whose members are
here referred to as "deutsche Polizei" although they are native
Viennese, had taken over power from the institutions of the
Vaterländische Front as represented by the slightly more
humane if cowardly constable:

*Stadtparkeingang von der Ringstraße. Hinter Bänken hohes
Eisengitter, das sich zum Stadtpark öffnet. Am Gittertor eine
auffallende Warnungstafel: JUDEN IST DER EINTRITT
VERBOTEN. Durchblick auf einen knospenden Fliederbusch. Im
Hintergrund mit fußhohen Gittern geschützte sprießende Beete,
Büsche, knospende Bäume. Sonniges Mittaprilwetter.*

*Auf dem Ring vorm Stadtparkeingang ein Auflauf.
Dichtgedrängte Zuschauermenge, die Rücken hergekehrt.
Gelächter, Gekicher, anfeuernde Rufe, hysterisches
Weibergequietsch.*

ERSTER PASSANT *aufbrüllend vor Lachen:* Jetz ist ihm der
    ganze Kübel voll Wasser übern Kopf, hahaha. Recht
    geschieht ihm. Patschnaß ist er.
EINE FRAU *kreischt ergötzt auf:* Der Glatzkopferte ist naß!
ZWEITER PASSANT: Schaun S' den guaten Anzug an, den er
    hat. Bestimmt vierhundert Schilling. Wettn mer?
ERSTER PASSANT: Wo hast denn die Schaln her, Saujud,
    verdächtiger? Gstohln, was?
WACHMANN *tritt von links auf:* Weitergehn – weitergehn! ...
    Kein Auflauf! Na, was is denn ...? Auseinandergehn.
    Gehn mer, gehn mer. Platz da!
EINE FRAU: Platz für die deutsche Polizei!

*Die Menge rückt auseinander, gewährt Ausblick auf die vier
jungen Burschen, drei davon in brauner SA-Uniform, einer in
schwarzen SS-Hosen, weißem Hemd, Hakenkreuzarmbinde,
mit Totenkopf-Emblem garnierter Schirmkappe. Auf dem
Trottoir rutschen drei Männer auf Knien umher, ihre Kleider
sind durchnäßt; Eimer, Lappen, Bürsten verstreut auf dem
nassen Trottoir. Zugleich wird die Ringstraßenbank links vom
Gittertor sichtbar, auf der zwei ältere Kleinbürgerinnen hocken
und unermüdlich stricken. Der Bursche im weißen Hemd
versetzt einem der Kriechenden einen laschen Tritt, stiefelt,
gefolgt von den drei SA-Leuten, schnell auf den Wachmann zu,
der sich umzingelt sieht.*

SS-MANN HANS BOCKERER *sanft, in versteckter Drohung*:
Paßt Ihnen hier vielleicht etwas nicht, Herr Inspektor?
WACHMANN: Gewiß, gewiß. Alles, alles. I hab mir nur
gedacht, so viele Menschen, ein Auflauf ... vielleicht ein
Unglücksfall...daß jemand schlecht gwordn is ...
ZWEITER SA-MANN: Aber ka Spur. Alles in Ordnung hier.
Wir ham nur die paar Saujuden zum Aufreiben
herbracht.
HANS BOCKERER: Die ganze Stadt is ja mit dena
Krukenkreuz verschandelt. Unser schönes Wien. Wanns
s' es aufmaln ham können, können s' es aa wegputzen.
Oder sind Sie vielleicht anderer Ansicht, Herr Inspektor?
WACHMANN *verlegen*: Aber woher denn. Aufgemalt, wegputzt.
Salutiert. Diener, meine Herren. Bitte äh – bittäh, sich
nicht inkommodieren zu lassen.
HANS BOCKERER *scharf*: Heil Hitler, Herr Inspektor!
WACHMANN *beflissen*: Heil Hitler, wie gesagt. Heil Hitler. *Eilig
rechts ab.*
EINE FRAU *kreischt*: Heil, die deutsche Sicherheitswache!
Fescher Kerl, der Herr Inspektor.
*Die drei auf den Knien Rutschenden haben die
Aufwischarbeit unterbrochen und aufgeguckt.*
HANS BOCKERER *fährt die hastig Weiterputzenden wütend
an*: Ja, wo san mer denn? Im Café Rebhuhn? Wer hat
euch die Erlaubnis gebn zum Unterbrechen, Gfriser,
elendiche – *Tritt einen der drei ins Gesäß; der Mann fällt
unterdrückt aufschreiend flach auf den Bauch. Gelächter.*
ERSTER PASSANT: Jetzt schwimmt er. *Gelächter.*
DER ZWEITE KNIENDE *hat sich langsam erhoben, ein
glatzköpfiger älterer Mann, mit Würde Hans Bockerer
anblickend*: Ich bitte – ich bitte –
HANS BOCKERER *schreit in dessen Gesicht*: W-a-s?
Widersprechen? Jetzt wirst was derleben, du Hund!
SS-MANN GSTETTNER *salopp*: Apportieren lassen, den Hund.
ZWEITER UND DRITTER SS-MANN *packen und werfen den
Glatzköpfigen flugs zu Boden.*
HANS BOCKERER *greift einen nassen Wischlappen und
versucht, ihn dem auf allen vieren Kauernden in den
Mund zu zwingen*: Nimm's Apportl ins Maul, du Hund.
*Da der Kauernde sich sträubt, klatscht Hans ihm den
nassen Fetzen über den Kopf, knüllt und zwingt ihn ihm
abermals zum Mund.* Nimm's Apportl ins Maul, du ...
Zitternd erschnappt der Glatzköpfige den Lappen.
SCHRILLE FRAUENSTIMME *aus der Menge*: Er kann ja, wenn
er wüll!
GSTETTNER *ist einige Schritte zur Seite getreten, klopft sich
zungenschlagend auf den Schenkel*: Ts-ts-ts, bring's
Apportl...Bring's Apportl, hab i gsagt ... *Vorgeneigt.* Na, kumm
schön, Hunderl ... *Zunehmendes Gekicher.*

HANS BOCKERER: Kannst denn net folgen, Sauhund? *Tritt den Kauernden ins Gesäß. Der Getretene kriecht mit dem Wischlappen im Mund auf allen vieren auf SS-Mann Gstettner zu.*

GSTETTNER: So ist brav, so ist brav. Na, gib schön's Apportl Jetz ... *Der ihm vor die Füße Gekrochene hebt langsam den Kopf, der Bursche reißt ihm den Lappen aus dem Mund, das anschwellende Gekicher der Umstehenden artet in ein allgemeines Lachgebrüll aus:* Braaaves Hunderl!

ERSTER PASSANT: Sagen S', kennen S' den net? Mir kommt sein Gesicht so bekannt vor.

ZWEITER PASSANT: Natürlich. Das ist der Gerstberger vom Deutschen Volkstheater. Der Komiker.

FRAUENSTIMME: Is er's? Der war aber guat. Über den ham mer oft Tränen glacht, über'n Gerstberger.

GSTETTNER *jovial:* Na, Volksgenossin, jetzt ham S' no mehr glacht, net?[129]

It would be a relief to be able to say that this presentation of street life in Vienna in the Spring of 1938 was sensationalist and exaggerated. If anything, it is understated. Jews were made to wash cars that had been expropriated from them by the SS or to clean out public toilets with their bare hands. Sometimes a caustic soda was added to the water to burn their skin. Viennese citizens queued up in front of the Schiller-Café to have their shoes polished free of charge by Jews. Jewish store-owners were dragged from their homes at night to open up their businesses, while trucks were lined up outside ready to load up the spoils. Titbits were thrown to the onlookers to keep them happy. While their shops were being plundered, Jewish grocers were placed on a barrel on the street and forced to eat raw potatoes. Jews were made to stand in two lines along the Reichsbrücke and to spit into each other's faces. (One young lad who refused to obey and declared that he would prefer to be shot was arrested and murdered a few weeks later in Dachau.) Jews were forced to do a goose march through the streets with sweeping brushes over their shoulders. Women were dragged out of their beds at night and made go on a "Judenspaziergang" in their night-dresses. Members of the Hitler Youth shaved off the beards of venerable old Rabbis in the street. The community house and synagogue in the Seitenstettengasse was occupied by SS men who forced members of the faithful to do knee-bends and press-ups, brutally kicking and beating those older and weaker Jews who could not keep up with the pace. Orthodox Jews were forced to lick pork blood off the floor of the Markthalle – in the Nazis' endless range of sadistic ideas, the element of sacrilege was an added spice. "Jetzt sank die Maske", wrote Carl Zuckmayer:

> Jetzt wurde nicht mehr bloß geraubt und gestohlen, sondern jedem privaten Rachegelüst freies Spiel gelassen. Mit nackten Händen mußten Universitätsprofessoren die Straßen reiben, fromme weißbärtige Juden wurden in den Tempel geschleppt und von johlenden Burschen gezwungen, Kniebeugen zu machen und im Chor "Heil Hitler" zu schreien. Man fing unschuldige Menschen auf der Straße wie Hasen zusammen und schleppte sie, die Abtritte der SA-Kasernen zu fegen; alles, was krankhaft schmutzige Haßphantasie in vielen Nächten sich orgiastisch ersonnen, tobte sich am hellen Tage aus. Daß sie in die Wohnungen einbrachen und zitternden Frauen die Ohrgehänge abrissen – dergleichen mochte sich bei Städteplünderungen vor hunderten Jahren in mittelalterlichen Kriegen ebenfalls ereignet haben; neu aber waren die schamlose Lust des öffentlichen Quälens, die seelischen Marterungen, die raffinierten Erniedrigungen.[130]

The poet Stella Rotenberg, writing in England in 1966, recalls the sudden invasions of brute force into the domestic sphere which were the daily lot of Jewish families in those times:

> Wer klopft?
> Warum klopft es in der Nacht?
> Ich weiß schon wer es ist, darum – nicht aufgemacht!
> Ich habe Angst. Meine Mutter steht
> auf aus dem Bett. Bis hin zur Türe geht
> sie wie ein Blindes. Sie will den Vater schützen.
> Aufs Türholz wird gehaut. Drei Mann mit Mützen,
> der Schirm verwegen auf den Nasenrücken,
> stürmen herein. Ich will mich bücken
> um nicht gesehn zu sein, da hör ich meine Mutter schrein,
> ich faß den einen Mann am Bein –
> seither hab ich die Schramme im Gesicht.[131]

Minna Lachs witnessed how at the end of April 1938 the SS cordoned off the Wohlmuthstraße and stood guard over a group of terrified Jewish men, women and boys. She slipped past and managed to reach home safely, only to hear later that evening that the group of rounded-up Jews had been driven screaming into the icy cold Danube. "Nur sehr gute Schwimmer konnten sich retten".[132] In a confidential report written by Leo Lauterbach for the Zionist Organization about his findings in Vienna between 18 and 21 April, the author details the violent house searches, "Entjudung" of businesses, mass arrests, deportations, but says that the public acts of sadism as described above had the most devastating effect on the morale of the Jewish community:

Obgleich eine augenscheinliche Nebensächlichkeit im Vergleich mit den anderen Handlungen unter dem neuen Regime, hatten doch die tiefste Wirkung auf die jüdische Bevölkerung das erzwungene Reiben von Gehsteigen, Waschen von Kasernen, etc. Nicht nur lähmte die Angst, solcher Frohn unterzogen zu werden, [...] sondern der Anblick der sich weidenden, verhöhnenden und schreienden nichtjüdischen Menge, hervorgerufen durch solche demütigende Vorstellungen, verursachte der gesamten jüdischen Bevölkerung einen furchtbaren Schock. Es beraubte die Juden jeden Gefühls persönlicher Sicherheit und ihres Glaubens an die Menschlichkeit der Nachbarn. Es enthüllte ihnen, daß sie nicht nur in einem Narrenparadies, sondern in einer wahren Hölle lebten. Niemand, der den Durchschnittswiener bis damals kannte, würde glauben, daß er auf eine solche Stufe sinken konnte.[133]

One report after another corroborates the eager complicity of the Viennese population in the acts of humiliation. Fred Wander wrote in his memoirs:

Immer wieder hörten wir, wie in Wien jüdische Geschäftsinhaber herausgeholt wurden, um mit eigener Hand das Hakenkreuz auf ihre Schaufenster zu pinseln oder das Wort *Judensau*, in großen weißen Lettern. Sie waren stets von belustigten Zuschauern umgeben, oft wurden die Scheiben eingeschlagen und die Läden geplündert. Viele zufällig vorbeikommende Leute, biedere Wiener, hatten dabei ihr Vergnügen. Jüdische Frauen und Männer mußten auf der Straße knien und das Pflaster säubern, umgeben von einer erheiterten Zuschauermenge. Die Polizei griff nicht ein. Ich selbst habe dieses Schauspiel in Wien mehrmals gesehen! Wilde Horden, oft angeführt von hysterisch geifernden Frauen, zogen durch die Straßen und zertrümmerten jüdische Geschäfte. Die Zuschauer lachten zufrieden und applaudierten.[134]

Needless to say, there were many non-Jewish citizens who were appalled by the excesses they were forced to witness on a day-to-day basis, but many lacked the courage to intervene on behalf of Jews in the face of the brash and triumphalist manner of the Nazis and Nazi sympathisers. The behaviour of many onlookers will have corresponded to Alois Vogel's description of a street scene in Klosterneuburg in his novel *Totale Verdunkelung*. The fictitious character Richard Wohlleben, a former officer of the *Heimwehr*, the military wing of the *Vaterländische Front*, is a secret opponent of Hitler's Anschluss. On the day after the so-called *Reichskristallnacht* he is part of the following scene, which is very telling in that it describes the mixed feelings of the onlookers, gives the lie to the frequently parroted anti-Semitic stereotyping of those times and exposes Wohlleben's own culpable evasiveness as well as the psychology of group pusillanimity, an essential factor in facilitating Nazism. It also shows how fascist audacity could dissolve when confronted by a decisive figure of authority:

Hitler-Jugend stand vor einigen Geschäften, die noch Juden gehörten. Bei manchen waren die Fensterscheiben zertrümmert und die Regale ausgeräumt. Bei Mayer, wo er [Wohlleben] seine Anzüge kaufte, hielten zwei Halbwüchsige den Besitzer unter dem Gejohle und der aufmunternden Assistenz von zehn bis fünfzehn jüngeren Burschen dazu an, mit Kalkfarbe, die sie offenbar mitgebracht hatten, auf die heilen Scheiben der Auslagen JUD und SAUJUD zu pinseln. Mayers Augen waren verschwollen, das Lid des rechten war blaurot unterlaufen, seine Kleidung war schmutzig. Der Mann zitterte am ganzen Leib. Einer der beiden Anführer – sie trugen beide schwarze Breeches zu ihren Braunhemden, auf deren Ärmeln Bänder mit der Aufschrift HJ-Streifendienst genäht waren – hatte eine Pistole in der Hand, der andere einen Hartgummiknüppel. Der mit dem Knüppel schrie: "Die Sara, wo ist die Sara! Die Sara muß her! Wir werden ihr den Judenstern auf den dicken Arsch tätowieren!" Die jüngeren Burschen lachten daraufhin und schrien im Sprechchor: "Sara! Sara! Sara!"

Wohlleben mußte sich beeilen, daß er "seinen" Autobus bekam. Warum eigentlich? Der nächste ging in fünfzehn Minuten und der nächste wieder in fünfzehn Minuten. Er hatte eine Dienststellung, die ihm gewisse Unabhängigkeit ließ, er wurde nicht kontrolliert. Kein Mensch sagte etwas, wenn er eine halbe Stunde später kam. Einige Sekunden zögerte er. "Sara! Sara! Sara! Sau-Jud! Sau-Jud! Sau-Jud!" tönte es von der anderen Straßenseite zu ihm herüber.

Einige Passanten waren stehengeblieben, schüttelten den Kopf, andere lachten. "Geschieht ihnen schon recht", hörte Wohlleben unmittelbar in seiner Nähe eine Stimme. "Diese jüdischen Blutsauger. Man weiß doch, welche Schinderlöhne die zahlen. Können leicht billiger sein als unsere arischen Kaufleute, wo sie unsre brave Mädeln ausbeuten. Für ein Butterbrot müssen sie arbeiten. Na, und der junge Chef nimmt sie natürlich ins Bett. Wer nicht will, kann sich um einen anderen Posten umschauen! Kennen wir doch, kennen wir doch alles!" Ein kleiner Mann sprach so zu den Umstehenden. "Jetzt muß ein End' damit sein. Höchste Zeit, daß man endlich ein End' damit macht". Er blickte im Kreis um.

"Jud! Jud! Sau-Jud!" tönte es wieder von drüben, und "Sara! Sara! Sara!"

Einige Passanten schlichen weiter. Mit geducktem Kopf, mit eingezogenen Schultern setzten sie ihren Weg fort. Andere lachten. Andere nickten zu den Worten des Mannes beifällig. Eine alte Frau mit einer Einkaufstasche sagte: "Aber das ist nicht recht, daß man willkürlich alle verfolgt. Es gibt doch auch Anständige unter ihnen, und überhaupt, der Mayer hat gar keinen Sohn". Warum sagte eigentlich ich nichts, dachte Wohlleben. Das Ganze ist doch eine Gemeinheit. Der alte Mayer sprach etwas zu dem Burschen mit der Pistole. Wohlleben konnte es nicht verstehen. Die Bande drüben schrie und johlte zu laut. Er sah, dem alten Mann liefen die Tränen über die Wangen. Er dachte daran, wie er noch als Kind mit der Mutter beim Mayer seinen ersten Anzug gekauft hatte, wie ihm Frau Mayer einen Riegel Schokolade geschenkt hatte, wie die Mutter mit Herrn Mayer gehandelt hatte, wie sie sich mit Herrn Mayer auf einen günstigen Preis geeinigt hatte, wie Herr Mayer gesagt hatte: Weil es der erste Anzug für den jungen Herrn ist". Zum ersten Mal hatte ihn jemand junger Herr genannt.

"Jud! Jud! Sau-Jud!" schrien sie drüben.

Den einen der Quälgeister kannte er. Er war der Sohn des Hauptschullehrers. Die Eltern waren nette Leute, als gut katholisch bekannt, sie gingen im Stift aus und ein. Der Autobus! Er mußte zu seinem Autobus zurechtkommen. Er ging also weiter. Da er aber bereits an der Straßenecke angelangt war, sah er den jungen Chorherrn auf die Gruppe der randalierenden Burschen zugehen und den Rädelsführer, den Sohn des Hauptschullehrers, ansprechen. Wohlleben war schon zu weit entfernt, um zu verstehen, was gesprochen wurde. Er merkte nur, daß die Burschen plötzlich still waren, der Angesprochene die Pistole in seiner Hosentasche verschwinden ließ, das Trüppchen sich zerstreute und der Pater mit Herrn Mayer allein ins Geschäft ging. Warum nicht ich, warum nicht ich? fragte er sich. Sein Autobus war schon fort, und er mußte mit dem nächsten fahren, in dem er gegenüber der alten Frau mit der Einkaufstasche zu sitzen kam. Er konnte ihr nicht ins Gesicht schauen. Er schämte sich. Dabei hatte sie ihn in der Menschenansammlung vielleicht gar nicht gemerkt.

Vorbeigehen, immer vorbeigehen. Es geht einen nichts an. Es sind immer die anderen. Man hat genug eigene Probleme, ist schließlich genug belastet, muß sich nicht noch in andere Dinge einmischen. Man ... Wer ist das? Ich, immer ich! Immer vorbeigegangen, dort, wo mich ein anderer gebraucht hätte, weil ihm Unrecht geschehen war und wo ich nur ehrlich und entschieden hätte auftreten brauchen, wie der Augustiner-Chorherr. Immer zwar dagegen gewesen, doch nichts dagegen gemacht, überhaupt nichts gemacht, immer alles laufen lassen.[135]

The above passage corresponds to historical reality insofar as the monks of Klosterneuburg formed a core of resistance and helped many victims. A true anecdote told by Gitta Sereny serves to demonstrate how effective isolated cases of intervention could be, given the sado-masochistic psychostructure of the fascist personality, which not only derives enjoyment from domination but equally obeys the reflex to subjugate itself to authority. Sereny shows how even two fifteen-year-old schoolgirls with sufficient resoluteness could disperse a crowd. Gitta and her friend Effie went for a walk through Vienna on 14 March:

> On the Graben, one of Vienna's loveliest streets, we came across a band of men in brown uniforms, wearing swastika armbands, surrounded by a large group of Viennese citizens, many of whom were laughing. As we drew near, I saw that in the middle of the crowd a dozen middle-aged people, men and women, were on their knees, scrubbing the pavement with toothbrushes. I recognized one of them as Dr Berggrün, our paediatrician, who had saved my life when I was four and had diphtheria. I had never forgotten that night; he had wrapped me again and again in cool, wet sheets, and it was his voice I had heard early that dawn saying, "*Sie wird leben*". (She will live.)
> Dr Berggrün saw me start towards one of the men in brown; he shook his head and mouthed, "No", while continuing to scrub with his toothbrush. I asked the uniformed men what they were doing; were they mad?
> "How dare you!" one of them shouted.
> "How dare *you*!" I shouted back, and told him that one of the men they were humiliating was a great physician, a saver of lives.
> Stunningly beautiful, her trained voice as clear as a bell, Elfie called out, "Is this what you call our liberation?"
> It was extraordinary: within two minutes, the jeering crowd had dispersed, the brown guards had gone, the "street cleaners" had melted away. "Never do that again", Dr Berggrün said to us sternly, his small, round wife next to him nodding fervently, her face sagging with despair and exhaustion. "It is very dangerous." They gassed them in Sobibor in 1943.[136]

The lamentable fact is that cases of such intervention were few and far between, although they might well have been effective if they had been frequent. The Nazi regime used Austria as a testing ground to see how far they could go in persecuting Jews and other minorities without the general populace taking concerted action against it or, on an international scale, without the Western Powers undertaking a military intervention on behalf of the victims. As soon became evident, the regime could go as far as it liked, and many Austrians became more than willing executioners, to quote the title of Daniel Goldhagen's controversial book.[136] The historian Gerhard Botz says:

> National Socialist anti-Jewish policy found widespread (if not total) support in Austria, especially in Vienna, whereas in large parts of Germany this was not the case. That this policy could be carried out with only general guidance from above was only possible because it was able to build on the deep-rooted traditions of a Catholic, and later partly secularized, anti-Semitism. In some measure the anti-Jewish policy of the Third Reich as a whole was actually given a lead and radicalized by the Austrian Nazis and those close to them, without actual racial-political tendencies or thoughts of physical destruction of the Jews being very prevalent among the non-Jewish population. In this way even anti-Semites who were anti-Nazi helped to make the Final Solution possible.[137]

An article in *Der völkische Beobachter* on 26 April, 1938, praised the Viennese for their radicalism in comparison with the Germans, quoting them as saying: "Darr Jud muß weg und sein Gerschtl [belongings] bleibt da!". The article went on to make perfectly clear what Nazism intended to do:

> Bis zum Jahre 1942 muß das jüdische Element in Wien ausgemerzt und zum Verschwinden gebracht sein. Kein Geschäft, kein Betrieb darf zu diesem Zeitpunkt mehr jüdisch geführt sein, kein Jude darf irgendwo noch Gelegenheit zum Verdienen haben, und mit Ausnahme der Straßenzüge, in denen die alten Juden und Jüdinnen ihr Geld – dessen Ausfuhr unterbunden ist – verbrauchen und aufs Sterben warten, darf im Stadtbild nichts davon zu merken sein.[...]
>
> Juden, laßt alle Hoffnung fahren, unser Organisationsnetz ist so dicht, daß ihr keine Lücke finden werdet, durch die ihr wieder an die Futtertröge und Fleischtöpfe Ägyptens schlüpfen werden könnt. Es gibt nur eine Möglichkeit: Emigrieren, so euch jemand aufnimmt.[138]

In his ironically titled memoir *Keine Zeit für Eichendorff. Chronik unfreiwilliger Wanderjahre* (1979), Egon Schwarz described his experiences of the new regime at the age of 16. He attempts to convey the sudden feeling of utter exposure to which Jewish citizens were now subjected:

> War die eine Quälerei langweilig geworden, so konnte man damit rechnen, daß die Henkersknechte eine andere erfanden. Im Aushecken von Unwürdigkeiten waren sie ungemein einfallsreich. Als keine Wahlplakate mehr zu entfernen und alle Kruckenkreuze von den Gehsteigen

gewaschen waren, wurden die jüdischen Geschäfte boykottiert, man mußte Schaufenster mit antisemitischen Parolen überkleben oder beschilderte Stangen hochhalten, um die Passanten vor dem Kaufen in jüdischen Läden zu warnen. Einen solchen zwischen zwei breitbeinig dastehenden SA-Männern hindurch zu betreten, hätte einen Heroismus bedurft, den kaum jemand aufbrachte. [...] Dazu kam eine Hetzkampagne in den Medien, vor allem den Zeitungen, in denen Juden jeder Gemeinheit und jedes Verbrechens bezichtigt wurden. Die *Kronenzeitung* brachte eine populäre Artikelserie unter dem Titel *Wie ich Antisemit wurde*, die ich mit morbider Neugierde las, um zu erfahren, daß der eine sich gegen die Juden gewandt hatte, weil ihm ein jüdischer Kaufmann schlechte Waren verkauft, ein anderer, weil er einen Juden eine Scheibe Brot und ein Stück Kuchen gleichzeitig hatte essen sehen. Es gab keine Behörde, keine Instanz, bei der man sich gegen eine Beleidigung hätte verwahren, wo man sich über die gröblichsten Rechtsverletzungen und körperlichen Ausschreitungen hätte beschweren können. Im Gegenteil, diese Dinge waren ja von Amts und Gesetzes wegen angeordnet oder wurden von den höchsten Stellen augenzwinkernd geduldet. Es war ein sonderbares Gefühl, plötzlich vogelfrei zu sein.[139]

Joseph Roth, who felt that what had typified Austria up to then was an "Elan zur Mischung", wrote on 19 March, 1938, from his exile in Paris these resonating words on the profound cultural ramifications of the Anschluss:

Eine Welt ist dahingeschieden, und die überlebende Welt gewährt der toten nicht einmal eine würdige Leichenfeier. Keine Messe und kein Kaddisch wird Österreich zugebilligt. Der Vatikan müßte alle Glocken lauten lassen, aber er ist ohnmächtig wie ein Synedrion und liefert sich obendrein jeden Tag mehr dem Getto aus. Die europäische Kulturwelt müßte sozusagen ein Begräbnis erster Klasse veranstalten, im wahrsten Sinne des Wortes: ein "Staatsbegräbnis"; aber sie gleicht einem Gelähmten, der im Rollstuhl Totenwache neben einem Katafalk halten soll. Der preußische Stiefel stampft über älteste europäische Saat. Den Stephansturm, dem ein paar Jahrhunderte lang der Halbmond erspart geblieben ist, wird bald das Hakenkreuz in ein Unwahrzeichen verwandeln. Unter dem milden Himmel, in dessen Wölbung und Wolken die Melodien Beethovens und Mozarts und Bruckners beinahe greifbar schweben, rattern von nun an die stählernen Vögel Deutschlands, die Raubgeier von Preußen, und über der Kapuzinergruft flattert die alte schwarz-weiß-rote Feindin. "Europa" scheint bis jetzt lediglich begriffen zu haben, daß ein kleines Land von einem großen unterjocht worden ist. "Europa" hat kaum eine Ahnung davon, daß hier eine ganz große Welt, konzentriert (und also von zehnfacher Spannkraft) in einem kleinen Raum und in einer Handvoll

Menschen, von einem hohlen, aber wuchtigen Ungetüm einfach zertreten worden ist: eine Welt von einer Un-Welt; ein Land von einem Un-Land; ein Staat von einem Un-Staat; der Mensch von Un-Menschen; ein Asyl für obdachlose Kultur von einem eisengepanzerten Dreck; die Heiterkeit von der Zucht; das Launige vom Unwirschen; das Lebensfrohe vom selbstmörderischen Masochismus. Über ein Land kam nicht die Sintflut, sondern die Kloake.[140]

3.3 Debarment

The Anschluss and its aftermath brought an abrupt change for the worse in the treatment of German Jews as well. As Richard Schifter has written:

> More than five years after the Nazi take-over, hundreds of thousands of Jews were still in Germany, hoping that they could weather the storm.

> The events in Austria after March 11, 1938 ended that illusion. Jews would be picked up in the streets and publicly humiliated. They would be arrested for no reason other than that they were Jews. Segregation was imposed in the public schools. As the weeks and months passed, the anti-Semitic measures became increasingly oppressive and brutal. They gradually spread from Austria to Germany proper. The gas chambers of Birkenau could not have been reasonably foreseen in light of the dismissal notices received by Jewish government officials and professors in Germany in 1933. They could have been foreseen in the light of the treatment accorded to Jews throughout Austria from 12 March, 1938 onward.[141]

The sadism found expression in spontaneous acts carried out by the SS, SA or so-called "Rollkommandos" formed by Viennese citizens with swastika armbands – to such an extent that German Wehrmacht officers sometimes intervened to prevent the worst excesses on the streets – or in official ordinances published in newspapers or on placards imposing restrictions on Jews. Stefan Zweig's ageing mother was one of those who were affected:

> Gleich eine der ersten Wiener Verfügungen hatte sie hart getroffen. Sie war mit ihren vierundachtzig Jahren schon schwach auf den Beinen und gewohnt, wenn sie ihren täglichen kleinen Spaziergang machte, immer nach fünf oder zehn Minuten mühseligen Gehens auf einer Bank an der Ringstraße oder im Park auszuruhen. Noch war Hitler nicht

acht Tage Herr der Stadt, so kam schon das viehische Gebot, Juden dürften sich nicht auf eine Bank setzen – eines jener Verbote, die sichtlich ausschließlich zu dem sadistischen Zweck des hämischen Quälens ersonnen waren. [...] einer alten Frau oder einem erschöpften Greis zu verweigern, auf einer Bank für ein paar Minuten Atem zu holen, dies war dem zwangstigen Jahrhundert und dem Manne vorbehalten, den Millionen als den Größten dieser Zeit anbeten.[142]

Soon Jews were also to be barred from pubs, cafés, theatres and cinemas, as well as being refused the right to bathe in public or sit down in trams. Jewish students were banned from the University of Vienna, where in particular Jewish women had excelled in disproportionately large numbers compared to their non-Jewish counterparts.

Children, too, were soon to be made feel the chill of the new wind. Willy Stern describes the first discriminatory measures:

Wir jüdischen Kinder hatten immer 15 Minuten später Schulbeginn, offenbar um uns von den anderen zu isolieren. Wir mußten durch ein separates Tor, und selbst die Toiletten der anderen – "arischen" – Schulkollegen durften wir nicht benutzen. Das mag heute unwesentlich erscheinen, hatte aber damals eine massiv deprimierende Wirkung auf uns.[143]

By April 1938 Jewish children could neither attend school nor take up an apprenticeship and suffered terribly under being debarred from recreational activities. Fritz Kleinmann recalled how dreadful it was for the young:

Wir durften keinen Fußballplatz mehr betreten! Wir durften in kein Kino mehr gehen! Jetzt hielten wir uns fast ständig zu Hause auf: vier Kinder, der Bruder war wesentlich jünger, in so einer kleinen Wohnung! Die Mutter hat uns nicht mehr auf die Gasse gelassen, weil sie Angst hatte, daß wir in eine Schlägerei verwickelt werden.[144]

In April 1939 an eleven-year-old Jewish girl in Vienna wrote these lines, precocious in their sense of despair, to her aunt:

Liebes Tantele, Du schreibst, wir sollen Gottvertrauen haben. Ich glaube nicht an Gott. Warum hat er uns so gestraft? Ich kann Dir nicht schildern, was wir mitgemacht haben. Mir hat Gott meine lieben Eltern genommen ... Ich darf in kein Kino gehen, in kein Theater, ich darf nicht in den Park gehen, manche Tage darf ich mich nicht auf den Straßen zeigen. Ist das nicht genug? Ich bin noch nicht ganz zwölf Jahre, aber manchmal glaube ich, daß ich schon hundert Jahre alt bin.[145]

This forced prematurity is touched upon in Ruth Klüger's account of her surreptitious visit to a cinema in the district of Hietzing. The passage is quoted at some length to convey the everyday deprivations, anxieties and confrontations suffered by Jewish children, as well as the way in which the non-Jewish youth tended to assume the denunciatory "Blockwart" mentality. Although Klüger was yet to undergo the horrors of Theresienstadt, Auschwitz and Christianstadt, this incident remained imprinted on her memory as a prologue to what was to come:

Es muß 1940 gewesen sein, ich war acht oder neun Jahre alt, im Kino um die Ecke wurde "Schneewittchen" gespielt. Der berühmte Walt Disney-Film läuft noch heute alle Jubeljahre mal in Amerikas großen Kinos, und wenn er auf dem Programm steht, ist es ein Volksfest für kleine wie für erwachsene Disneyfans. Ich bin seit meinem ersten Micky-Maus-Film, den ich noch vor dem Anschluß mit dem Kindermädel in einer Nachmittagsvorstellung innigst genoß, sehr gern ins Kino gegangen, und so wollte ich auch diesen Film unbedingt sehen, durfte aber als Jüdin leider nicht hinein. Darüber klagte und schimpfte ich abwechselnd, bis meine Mutter vorschlug, daß ich doch einfach gehen sollte und basta.

Es war Sonntag, wir waren in der Nachbarschaft bekannt, hier ins Kino zu gehen, war eine Herausforderung. Meine Mutter war der Überzeugung, daß niemand sich darum kümmern würde, ob ein Kind mehr oder weniger im Saal säße, und gab mir zu verstehen, daß ich mich einerseits zu wichtig nehme, andererseits beschämend feig sei. Das konnte ich nicht auf mir sitzen lassen, zog also drauf los, wählte die teuerste Platzkategorie, eine Loge, um nicht aufzufallen, und kam gerade dadurch neben die neunzehnjährige Bäckerstochter von nebenan und ihre kleinen Geschwister zu sitzen, eine begeisterte Nazifamilie.

Ich habe diese Vorstellung ausgeschwitzt und hab nie vorher oder nachher so wenig von einem Film mitbekommen. Ich saß auf Kohlen, vollauf mit der Frage beschäftigt, ob die Bäckerstochter wirklich böse zu mir hinschielte, oder ob es mir doch nur so vorkäme. Die Niederträchtigkeiten von Schneewittchens Stiefmutter verschwammen mir auf der Leinwand zu einem vorgekauten Brei unechter Schlechtigkeit, während ich und keine Prinzessin im wahren, triefenden Fettnäpfchen saß, umzingelt.

Warum bin ich nicht aufgestanden und weggegangen? Vielleicht, um mich meiner Mutter nicht zu stellen oder weil ich meinte, gerade durchs Aufstehen und Weggehen Aufmerksamkeit zu erregen, vielleicht nur, weil man nicht aus dem Kino geht, bevor der Film aus ist, oder am wahrscheinlichsten, weil ich vor Angst nicht denken konnte. Ich weiß ja nicht einmal, warum wir alle nicht rechtzeitig aus Wien weg sind, und vielleicht gibt es eine Familienverwandschaft zwischen dieser Frage und meinem Kinoproblem.

Als es im Saal hell wurde, wollte ich die anderen vorgehen lassen, aber meine Feindin stand und wartete. Ihre kleinen Geschwister wurden ungeduldig, die Große sagte "Nein, seid's stad" und sah mich streng an. Die Falle war, wie gefürchtet, zugeschnappt. Es war der reine Terror. Die Bäckerstochter zog ihre Handschuhe an, pflanzte sich endlich vor mir auf, und das Ungewitter entlud sich.

Sie redete fest und selbstgerecht, im Vollgefühl ihrer arischen Herkunft, wie es sich für ein BDM-Mädel schickte, und noch dazu in ihrem feinsten Hochdeutsch: "Weißt du, daß deinesgleichen hier nichts zu suchen hat? Juden ist der Eintritt ins Kino gesetzlich untersagt. Draußen steht's beim Eingang an der Kasse. Hast du das gesehen?" Was blieb mir übrig, als die rhetorische Frage zu bejahen?

Das Märchen vom Schneewittchen läßt sich auf die Frage reduzieren, wer im Königsschloß etwas zu suchen hat und wer nicht. Die Bäckerstochter und ich folgten der vom Film vorgegebenen Formel. Sie, im eigenen Hause, den Spiegel ihrer rassischen Reinheit vor Augen, ich, auch an diesem Ort beheimatet, aber ohne Erlaubnis, und in diesem Augenblick ausgestoßen, erniedrigt und preisgegeben. Ich hatte mich unter Vorspiegelungen falscher Tatsachen hier eingeschlichen, den Nazivers bestätigend: "Und der Jud hat den Brauch, / Und es bringt ihm was ein, / Schmeißt man vorne ihn aus, / Kehrt er hinten wieder rein". Wenn ich auch das Gesetz, das ich verletzt hatte, für ungerecht hielt, so war ich doch beschämt, ertappt worden zu sein. Denn die Scham entsteht einfach dadurch, daß man einer verbotenen Tat überführt wird, und hat oft mit schlechtem Gewissen gar nichts zu tun. Wäre ich nicht erwischt worden, so wäre ich auf meine Waghalsigkeit stolz gewesen. So war es umgekehrt: Man sieht sich im Spiegel boshafter Augen, und man entgeht dem Bild nicht, denn die Verzerrung fällt zurück auf die eigenen Augen, bis man ihr glaubt und sich selbst für verunstaltet hält. Das hat W.B. Yeats, Irlands größter Lyriker, in Versen geschrieben, und hätte ich die Zeilen über den "mirror of malicious eyes" nicht erst zehn Jahre später auswendig gelernt, so wäre mir vielleicht wohler gewesen.

Es ging dann doch schneller vorbei als erwartet, für mich immer noch lang genug. Der Vertreterin unanfechtbarer Gesetzlichkeiten fiel nicht mehr viel ein. Wenn ich mich noch ein einziges Mal unterstehen tät, hierher zu kommen, so würde sie mich anzeigen, ich hätt ja noch ein Glück, daß sie's nicht gleich täte. Ich stand mit weit aufgerissenen Augen, einigermaßen erfolgreich meine Tränen schluckend. Die Platzanweiserin, die zugehört hatte, denn wir waren die letzten im Saal, half mir nachher in den Mantel, drückte mir meine Geldbörse, die ich sonst liegen gelassen hätte, in die Hand und sagte ein paar beruhigende Worte. Ich nickte, unfähig zur Gegenrede, dankbar für den Zuspruch, eine Art Almosen.

Es war noch hell, ich lief ein wenig durch die Straßen, wie betäubt. Ich hatte an diesem Nachmittag für meine Person, in meinem Bereich und ganz unmittelbar erfahren, wie es mit uns und den Nazis stand. Daß der Schrecken in diesem Fall nicht ganz ungerechtfertigt war, änderte nichts an der Tatsache, daß ich es nun wußte. Ich hatte das Gefühl gehabt, in tödlicher Gefahr zu schweben, und dieses Gefühl verließ mich nicht mehr, bis es sich bewahrheitete. Ohne es richtig durchdenken zu müssen, war ich von jetzt an den Erwachsenen voraus.[146]

Jews were banned from sports activities. Already on 17 March, 1938, two days after Hitler's Heldenplatz speech, the football team "Austria" was disbanded because at least half of the players and all of the management were Jewish, and also because they cultivated a playful, decorative style of football, referred to by the Viennese as "Scheiberlspiel", which the Nazi authorities found to be inimical to the "Germanic" concept of sport. Players and managers had to flee the country, and a German military barracks was built on the site of their stadium. The team was revived under the name "Ostmark" but was severely weakened by the expulsion of its Jewish members. One of Vienna's most popular soccer-players, the non-Jewish Mathias Sindelar, quit the team, and on 23 January, 1939, he committed suicide along with his Jewish girlfriend Camilla Castagnola.[147] The story is told in Friedrich Torberg's "Auf den Tod eines Fußballspielers", written in the style of a street ballad to lend it a broadly appellative character and given unity by the "football game = life" conceit throughout:

Er war ein Kind aus Favoriten
und hieß Mathias Sindelar.
Er stand auf grünem Plan inmitten,
weil er ein Mittelstürmer war.

Er spielte Fußball und er wußte
vom Leben außerdem nicht viel.
Er lebte, weil er leben mußte,
Vom Fußball fürs Fußballspiel.

Er spielte Fußball wie kein zweiter,
er stak voll Witz und Phantasie.
Er spielte lässig, leicht und heiter.
Er spielte stets. Er kämpfte nie.

Er warf den blonden Schopf zur Seite,
ließ seinen Herrgott gütig sein,
und stürmte durch die grüne Weite
und manchmal bis ins Tor hinein.

Es jubelte die Hohe Warte,
der Prater und das Stadion,
wenn er den Gegner lächelnd narrte
und zog ihm flinken Laufs davon –

bis eines Tags ein andrer Gegner
ihm jählings in die Quere trat,
ein fremd und furchtbar überlegner,
vor dem's nicht Regel gab noch Rat.

Von einem einzigen, harten Tritte
fand sich der Spieler Sindelar
verstoßen aus des Planes Mitte,
weil das die neue Ordnung war.

Ein Weilchen stand er noch daneben,
bevor er abging und nachhaus.
Im Fußballspiel, ganz wie im Leben,
war's mit der Wiener Schule aus.

Er war gewohnt zu kombinieren,
und kombinierte manchen Tag.
Sein Überblick ließ ihn erspüren,
daß seine Chance im Gashahn lag.

Das Tor, durch das er dann geschritten,
lag stumm und dunkel ganz und gar.
Er war ein Kind aus Favoriten
und hieß Mathias Sindelar.[148]

3.4 The plebiscite

On the occasion of the plebiscite on "reunification" with the German Reich on 10 April, 1938, the result was a massive 99.73% for the Anschluss, partially as a result of brilliantly orchestrated propaganda leading up to it, the systematic intimidation of voters, exclusion of that 8% of the voting population which consisted of Jews and the "politically unreliable", but also undeniably due to the newly found and widespread Austrian enthusiasm for "die Wiedergeburt Großdeutschlands". Wilhelm Szabo deplored the outcome with these terse words:

Nach dem Entscheid

(10 April 1938)

Wir haben die Willkür erkoren.
Wir haben die Schande bejaht.
Wir haben das Echte verschworen,
bekräftigt Gemeinheit, Verrat.

Wir würdigten, die uns bestahlen.
Wir küßten die Hand, die uns schlug.
Wir fanden das Nein nicht zu Qualen,
zu Unrecht und hämischem Fug.

Keine Probe ward schlechter bestanden.
Wir haben uns selbst widersagt.
Wir schmückten die Schmach mit Girlanden.
Wir jubelten, wo man beklagt.[149]

But the prevalent mood of euphoria is undoubtedly better conveyed by the exalted tone of the National Socialist poet Max Mell, who declaimed on 10 April, again drawing grotesquely on religious phraseology:

Wir treten an, Bekenntnis abzulegen.
Ernst laßt uns großen Augenblick erwägen
und ihn zutiefst mit ganzem Herzen fassen:
Denn heut ersteht, wovon wir nicht mehr lassen.
Ja, unsrer Heimatlande lichter Reigen
will heim ins Reich, dem sie von je zu eigen,
dem sie sich nie entfremdet in den Zeiten,
und unser Wort darf sie zurückgeleiten.
Gewaltiger Mann, wie können wir dir danken?
Wenn wir von nun an eins sind ohne Wanken. [...]

Wir treten an, Bekenntnis abzulegen.
Wir wollen eins sein. Herr, gib du den Segen![150]

Or Joseph Georg Oberkofler in his undisguisedly racist hymn "Zum 10. April":

O deutsches Herz, voll Licht und Kraft und Glaube,
du, stets bewegt in deiner ewigen Ruh,
du bist der Adler und du bist die Taube,
und alle deutschen Stämme sind wie du.
Der Führer ruft. Tritt an in blanker Wehr!
Bekenne dich zu deinem Blute heut!
Denn dieser Tag trägt so wie keiner mehr
das große Volksreich in die Ewigkeit.[151]

As Franz Kain wrote of the extraordinary result of the plebiscite:

Die es beschönigen wollten, behaupteten stets, es habe keine Möglichkeit der Gegenpropaganda gegeben und es seien schon Tausende in den Konzentrationslagern gewesen und dazu sei noch eine riesige Maschinerie eingesetzt gewesen. Das alles ist richtig, aber es reicht zur Erklärung weder der hohen Wahlbeteiligung noch für den hohen Prozentsatz an Ja-Stimmen hin. Die Wahrheit ist, daß der Großteil der Bevölkerung in diesem Monat April tatsächlich für den Anschluß war, weil er sich davon ein besseres Leben versprochen hat.[152]

3.5 Dismissal, confiscation and eviction

In the period to follow, one of the reasons for the continued Viennese fervour for Nazism was that it "solved" the acute problems of unemployment and the lack of housing. The "Deutsche Arbeiterfront", the "gleichgeschaltete" Nazi trade union, ordered that all of Vienna's working Jews should be sacked by 30 June, 1938, to make way for the city's 200,000 unemployed "Aryans". The eviction of Jewish householders and tenants from their homes would make 70,000 extra dwellings available in Vienna alone. In 1941 Jews were banned from the use of public transport, of lifts in public buildings, telephone kiosks or hairdressers, and had to forfeit their spectacles, electrical gadgets, bicycles and winter clothing. They were no longer allowed to keep pets or buy newspapers or journals other than the *Jüdisches Nachrichtenblatt*. When rationing began, Jews were allowed no meat, eggs or milk. In September, 1941, the wearing of a yellow star and in April, 1942, the display of a star on one's apartment door was made obligatory. The regime made a profit from this act of humiliation, as Elizabeth Welt Trahan tells:

> You had to pay ten *Reichspfennig* for the star, and you were allowed to purchase only three together. Right over the heart it went, with *Jude* emblazoned in its center in large black letters, as if to mark the spot for Hagen's spear.[153]

Even if Elizabeth Welt Trahan, though Jewish, did not have to wear the yellow star as the citizen of a friendly power, Romania, the humiliation connected with it was brought home to her one day when she tried out wearing one belonging to a Jewish friend. Her account of what happened is a condemning document of Viennese *Alltagsgeschichte*:

> One time Ditha forgot her jacket at my place. For a while I studied its bright yellow star, then I put it on and went out. While I was in our neighbourhood I covered the star with my purse, then I bared it. I wanted to know what it felt like – perhaps I also wanted in some minor way to make amends for my priliveged status.
>
> It was an unnerving experience. I may have imagined it, but it seemed to me that everybody was either staring at me as if I were a freak, or looking away deliberately, pretending that I didn't exist. In a defiant mood I stopped an older woman and asked for directions to a nearby street. "I don't know," she mumbled and hurried off. Two teenagers smirked and said something as I was passing. Though I didn't catch the meaning, I was sure that the remark had been pejorative and directed at me.
>
> I stopped at a shop window, not to glance at its display but because I was startled to see my reflection wearing a star. As if I as a non-Jew was seeing a Jew for the first time, and also seeing myself for the first time as a Jew. Then I noticed that a saleslady inside was motioning me to move on. She had an angry, mean face. I began to cross a small park, but when I saw the sign ONLY FOR ARYANS on the nearest park bench I quickly retraced my steps. In my hurry to get home I forgot to cover the star. I rushed upstairs in a sweat and tore off the jacket. I felt like an escaped convict, subhuman, branded. How could my friends stand it, how could they live in this city and among these people day after day, and not lose their self-respect or become violent?
>
> Just then the doorbell rang. I hid the jacket in case it was Inge but it was Ditha, its owner. With amazing equanimity she picked it up, put it on, star showing, and left.[154]

By 1942 an additional tenth of the total of Vienna's dwellings had been made available to "Aryans" by the wholesale eviction of Jewish tenants and owners. Theodor Kramer, the popular nature poet who more than anyone else had made the landscape of the Weinviertel north of Vienna his theme and was now banned from publishing and was hunted from flat to flat with his family, wrote of the incomprehensible changes in his own status as a citizen and a human, as well as of the pain of not being allowed to order a drink in a beer garden, sit on a bench or, worst of all, witness the burgeoning of plants in spring:

Blühst du noch immer, kleiner Baum
im Vorstadtpark am Rasensaum?
Die Leut gehaben sich ringsum
ganz anders, und ich selbst geh stumm.
Ja, kleiner Baum, du blühst noch.

Grünst du noch immer, gutes Gras?
Seit langem trink ich schon kein Glas,
verschlossen ist mir jeder Schrank,
kein Platz für mich ist auf der Bank.
Ja, grünes Gras, du blühst noch.

Reifst du noch immer, harte Beer?
Ein Jahr nur, Stemplein, ist es her,
da galt ich was und war ein Mann,
doch heute schlägt mir nichts mehr an.
Ja, harte Beer, du reifst noch.

Gegrüßt seid, Baum und Gras und Beer,
ihr seid noch da, ich dank euch sehr.
Wenn ich auch stumm vorübergeh
und übers Jahr euch nicht mehr seh,
ihr blüht und grünt und reift noch.[155]

These decrees forbidding Jews to set foot in any public gardens and parks had begun in June 1938. The only place left to them and their children for recreation − a truly necrophilic inspiration on the part of the Nazis and a signalling of their ultimate intentions − was the Jewish section of the Vienna's main cemetery, the Zentralfriedhof, some seven kilometers from the centre of the city. In her novel *Die größere Hoffnung*, Ilse Aichinger describes the perturbing experience of playing as a child in these literally and metaphorically cryptic surroundings:

Dieser letzte Friedhof war tief von verzweifelten Geheimnissen, von Verwunschenheiten, und seine Gräber waren verwildert. Es gab da kleine, steinerne Häuser mit fremden Buchstaben darauf und Bänken, um zu trauern,

aber es hatte auch Schmetterlinge und Jasmin gegeben,
solange es Sommer war, und ein Unmaß von Verschwiegenem
und wachsenden Sträuchern über jedem Grab. Es tat weh,
hier zu spielen, und jeder schnelle, übermütige Schrei
verwandelte sich sofort in abgründige Sehnsucht.[156]

In his poem "Der gute Ort zu Wien", Franz Werfel wrote of the
paradox of the sudden appearance of so much family activity
in the arena of death. The following is an excerpt:

Volksgarten, Stadt- und Rathauspark,
Ihr Frühling war noch nie so stark.
Den Juden Wiens ist er verboten.
Ihr einziges Grün wächst bei den Toten.

Zur Stunde, da die Stadt erblaßt
Vor sonntäglicher Mittagslast,
Drückt es sich scheu in Straßenbahnen
Hinaus zu halbvergessnen Ahnen.

Der Totenstadt von Simmering
Sind Christ und Jud das gleiche Ding,
Verschieden nur durch Zins und Kosten.
Die Juden wohnen gegen Osten.

Das hohe Tor steht offen halb,
Der Tag ist grell, der Jud ist falb.
Das kommt, so seltsam abgetragen,
Mit Weib und Kind und Kinderwagen.

In Väterzeiten lang verdorrt,
Da hieß der Friedhof: "Guter Ort".
Nun ist, als Schutz vor feigen Horden,
Zum guten Ort er wieder worden.

Auf seinen Wegen und Alleen
Herrscht großes Kommen, großes Gehn,
Als würden alle, hier begraben,
In diesen Tagen Jahrzeit haben.

Man liest die Namen neu und alt,
Umdrängt der Steine Rundgestalt,
Und zu den streng erstaunten Steinen
Dringt Sorgenschwatz und Kinderweinen.[157]

Another reason for intensified activity in the Zentralfriedhof
was the sudden increase in Jewish deaths. According to
official statistics, there were in all 213 suicides in Vienna in
March 1938 – three times the monthly average – and 138 in
April. Of these, 79 in March and 62 in April (as against 4 in
February) were Jewish. It is probable that many of these so-
called suicides were actually murders perpetrated on the
streets or in prison cells by Nazi sadists who were never to be

brought to justice for their deeds. Erich Fried's father, Hugo Fried, met such a fate. In their preparations for flight from Vienna, Fried's parents arranged a meeting of friends in the Café Thury below their flat in the Alserbachstraße on 24 April. This must have been reported immediately to the police as the parents were arrested on the same evening on the charge of "Vorbereitung zur Devisenverschiebung ins Ausland". Hugo Fried was held in "protective detention" for a month and was brought home on 24 May after a Gestapo interrogation, almost exactly on his forty-eighth birthday. At first, Erich Fried failed to recognize his father, who had been so maltreated that his hair had turned from black to white within a month:

Als man ihn nach Hause brachte, gegen Mittag des Tages, an dessen Abend er starb, traf ich ihn, während man ihn die Treppen hinaufschleppte, und erkannte ihn zuerst nicht, sondern glaubte, als ich unsere Nachbarin neben dem röchelnden alten Mann sah, er gehörte irgendwie zu ihr, und der Polizist und der Chauffeur, die diesen sterbenden Menschen von Stufe zu Stufe hinaufhoben, hätten nur mit ihr, nichts mit mir und meiner Großmutter zu tun. Ich erinnere mich noch meiner Erleichterung darüber. Als ich unsere Nachbarin, die offenbar schon mit den beiden Männern gesprochen hatte und nun weinend mitging, fragte, ob ich etwas für sie tun könne, packte sie mich am Arm und sagte: "Wissen Sie nicht, wer das ist? Das ist Ihr Vater!"

Ein Gestapobeamter, Herr Göttler, später in der Bundesrepublik Zollrat in Düsseldorf, hatte ihm einige Tage zuvor die Magenwand eingetreten.

Vielleicht waren es die weißen Bartstoppeln, die mich gehindert hatten, meinen Vater im mehr als halbdunkeln Treppenhaus auf den ersten Blick zu erkennen. Ich hatte ihn nie anders als glattrasiert gesehen. Und das letzte Mal, am Tag seiner Verhaftung, genau einen Monat vor seinem Tod, hatte er noch keine grauen oder gar weißen Haare gehabt. Als ich ihn dann, drei Tage später, im offenen Sarg, wiedersah, war er rasiert worden und sah etwas besser aus, als sei der Tod eine Erholung für ihn gewesen.[158]

Erich Fried, then seventeen years of age and, like all members of his ethnic group, allowed to go strolling only in the Jewish section of the graveyard in Simmering, was struck by the same paradox of *vita in morte* as in Zweig's "Der gute Ort zu Wien":

Am Judenfriedhof ist viel Land umbrochen
und Sarg um Sarg kommt, und die Sonne scheint.
Der Pfleger sagt: So geht es schon seit Wochen.
Ein Kind hascht Falter, und ein Alter weint.

Dumpft fällt der Vater in die Erde,
ich werfe Lehm nach, feucht und kalt.
Der Kantor singt. Es wiehern schwarze Pferde.
Es riecht nach Sommeraufenthalt.

Die mir die Gärten meiner Stadt versagen,
die Bank im staubigen Grün am Kai,
sie haben mir den Vater totgeschlagen,
daß ich ins Freie komm und Frühling seh.[159]

The situation in Vienna was so fraught with danger that those who had managed to emigrate in time were actually relieved to hear that a relative or dear friend had died of more or less natural causes before the Nazi system could do away with them. Stefan Zweig wrote of his mother Ida, who died a few months after the Nazi occupation:

Und ich schäme mich nicht, zu sagen – so hat die Zeit unser Herz pervertiert – , daß ich nicht erschrak, als die Nachricht vom Tode meiner Mutter kam, die wir in Wien zurückgelassen hatten, sondern daß ich im Gegenteil sogar eine Art Beruhigung empfand, sie vor allen Leiden und Gefahren nun gesichert zu wissen.[160]

Only in this extraordinary context can one rightly comprehend the seemingly oedipal title of Theodor Kramer's poem "Ich bin froh, daß du schon tot bist, Vater". According to Kramer, his father Dr Max Kramer died in December 1935 as he had always wished to: in his favourite café while playing cards. The first stanza reads:

Ich bin froh, daß du schon tot bist, Vater,
daß du starbst, bevor die Horde kam,
die mich schrubben ließ, die mir im Prater
am Kastanienblust die Freude nahm.
Ich bin froh, daß dich zum Spaß kein Bube
zerrte je am langen weißen Bart,
daß man dich nicht bannte in die Stube;
denn viel auszugehn war deine Art.[161]

The poem "Erster Spaziergang nach der Verfolgung" by Friedrich Bergammer, who like some 80,000 fellow-Austrian Jews was forced into exile in 1938, was written in the freedom of New York, but indicates how the Nazi terror tactics continued to paralyse their victims for a long time afterwards. The text deals with the psychological consequences of such measures even when they are firmly consigned to the past, the triplet stanzas conveying the poet's gingerly attempts to come to terms with civil liberty, the single lines the relapse into inbred anxiety:

Nicht auf einmal will ich es genießen,
in den schönen Sommerpark zu gehn.
Ach, ich muß zuerst die Augen schließen

und dann will etwas weiter sehn
in das mir erlaubte, grüne Land,
wo um Bäume ihre Stillen stehn,

geh' nicht allzufern vom Gartenrand.

Eh' ich wag, die Schatten auszuloten,
muß ich an die ferne Tafel denken:
Juden ist der Eintritt hier verboten!

Und die weiße Aufschrift auf den Bänken:
Nur für Arier. Dann erst mag die Hand
sich von den geschloss'nen Augen senken,

doch mein Blick geht nicht zu weit ins Land.

Und es tröstet nun, daß Häuserblöcke
neben den Geländern riesig säumen
diesen Garten eine lange Strecke.

Zögernd will ich in den Sonnenräumen
an der breiten Wiesendünung Strand
weiter gehen zu den hohen Bäumen,

nah dem Gitter und der Häuserwand.[162]

The same theme of traumatization appears in the poem "Nun da ich schweb im Ätherboot (1938)" by Hermann Broch, who, after three weeks imprisonment in Alt Aussee, felt that jail was like paradise compared to the terror of daily life in Vienna.[163] He was able through James Joyce's mediation to obtain an exit visa and fly out from Aspern on 24 July 1938 to Croydon. The poem tells in the first two lines of heaving a sigh of relief at the moment of lifting off into the air above Vienna, but the treble repetitions of the short lines in the first and second stanzas – "Da packt sie mich / Da packt sie mich / Da packt sie mich" and "Ich spürte bloß / Ich spürte bloß / Ich spürte bloß" – convey a shortness of breath caused by a panic attack even after the moment of escape. The image "Strich", the line drawn by the road beneath, is repeated an obsessive three times, echoing "den Schlingen*strich* / Den um den Hals ich trug", and stretching through the countryside parallel to the "steely flight" of the plane is the noose of fear accompanying the poet on his way to England. The last five lines express the age-old idea that, even in times of the greatest turbulence, the peasant reaps and sows and perpetuates the cycle of growth; but the last two stanzas also register a feeling which, through one-and-a-half centuries of anti-Semitic propaganda, had been presented as a contradiction in terms: the longing of a Jewish person for his/her soil, the emotional landscape, the "Heimat", in which he/she grew up.

> Nun da ich schweb im Ätherboot
> Und ich aufatmen kann,
> Da packt sie mich
> Da packt sie mich
> Da packt sie mich noch einmal an
> Die rohe Flüchtlingsnot.
>
> Ein Herz, das mir zum Abschied schlug
> Blieb ohne Trost zurück
> Ich spürte bloß
> Ich spürte bloß
> Ich spürte bloß den Schlingenstrick
> Den um den Hals ich trug.
>
> Da drunten ist nun nichts mehr groß
> Die Straße ist ein Strich
> Doch plötzlich weiß ich von dem Moos
> Und weiß den Wald, des Harz ich riech
> Und weiß, da drunten lag einst ich,
> Und lag in meiner Heimat Schoß
> Die weiße Straße ist ein Strich.
>
> Wie pfeilgrad endlos ist der Strich,
> Hier ist nur stählernes Gebraus
> Pfeilgrade geht der Flug
> Dort drunten steht ein Bauernhaus
> Ich weiß, dort drunten geht ein Pflug
> Ganz still und langsam, schnell genug
> Für's stille Brot, jahrein, jahraus.
> Pfeilgrad und stählern geht der Flug.[164]

4. The Holocaust begins

4.1 Deportation and execution

Those who did not manage to escape from Austria by early 1938 were soon to undergo the most unimaginable hardships. The deportations in Austria had begun only two weeks after the Heldenplatz speech. The first train left for Dachau concentration camp with 151 "detainees" (60 of them Jewish) on 1 April, the second with 120 (50 Jewish) on May 23. Dr Fritz Bock, former Vice-Chancellor, described how they were treated:

> Dann bogen die Wagen auf das Verschubgelände hinter dem Gebäude des Westbahnhofs ein und hielten; die Türen wurden aufgerissen: "Heraus, ihr Hunde!" Und es begann ein Spießrutenlaufen, an dessen Ende, oft erst nach Jahren, für viele der Tod stand. Durch eine Masse von SS-Bütteln, die mit dem Gewehrkolben mit aller Gewalt auf uns eindroschen, hieß es zu den Eisenbahnwaggons laufen ... Gegen Mitternacht setzte sich der Zug in Bewegung und damit begann bis in die Vormittagsstunden des 1. April eine wahrhaft unvergeßliche Fahrt, bei der sich die Angehörigen der Elite der NSDAP, meistens kräftige junge Burschen, abwechselnd an uns müde prügelten. Viele von uns hatten am Ende dieser "Reise" so zerschlagene Gesichter, daß sie nicht mehr einem menschlichen Antlitz glichen. Als nach fast zwölfstündiger Fahrt der Verschubbahnhof vor dem Dachauer Lager erreicht war, war es nur mehr eine taumelnde Masse menschlicher Kreaturen, die dann vor dem Kommando-gebäude des Dachauer Lagers Aufstellung nehmen mußte.[165]

Alfred Maleta, a former functionary of the *Vaterländische Front*, has a similar story to tell:

> Am 13. März 1938, am Nachmittag, wurde ich dann verhaftet, und am Fronleichnamstag 1938 nach Dachau gebracht. Wir fuhren mit dem letzten der drei berüchtigten Österreich-Transporte, mit denen die gesamte Führungsschicht des österreichischen Staates nach Dachau befördert wurde. Seit Jahren bestand in München eine eigene Gestapo-Leitstelle für Österreich, in der die politischen Persönlichkeiten des immerhin noch souveränen Staates gleich Kriminellen oder innerstaatlichen Hochverrätern registriert waren. Auf Befehl dieser Gestapo-Leitstelle waren wir verhaftet worden und traten jetzt eine Reise in die Unterwelt an. Bereits beim

Aussteigen aus dem "grünen Heinrich" begann ein Spießrutenlauf vom Bahnhofsvorplatz bis zum Einstieg in die Waggons durch ein Spalier der Dachauer SS, bedacht mit Fußtritten und Gewehrkolbenhieben. Wir marschierten in das Lager ein, genau in jenem Augenblick, als das gesamte Lager zum Appell antrat. Da taumelten gerade der ehemalige Präsident des Gewerkschaftsbundes, Kollege Staud, und sein Mitarbeiter Troidl den Weg entlang. Sie schleppten einen jener schweren gußeisernen Suppenkessel, deren Gewicht und dünne Henkel einem fast die Finger abschnitten.[166]

Leo Jagoda, a Jewish trader from Graz, told of how, when new groups were lined up before the headquarters of the camp, an SS man read out the regulations, which included the passage: "Selbstmord ist gestattet, aber er muß tot sein, sonst wird der Mann bestraft".[167] The journalist Rudolf Kalmar describes the public floggings of inmates who had committed some trivial misdemeanour. The new Austrian contingent was forced to watch the punishment rituals to see what was in store for them:

Zwei robuste SS-Leute zogen umständlich die Feldblusen aus, schoben die Hemdsärmel hoch und griffen sich aus dem Kübel voll Wasser je einen geschmeidigen Ochsenziemer heraus. Ein paar durch die Luft gezogene Hiebe knallten wie schwere Pistolen.

Dann wurde ein Mann, ein schlanker Bursche aus einem reichsdeutschen Block, aufgerufen, der lief, so schnell die Beine ihn tragen konnten, zum Bock. Die SS-Leute schnallten ihn fest und verprügelten ihn. Einer von rechts und einer von links. Jeder Schlag, der sich tief in das Fleisch fraß, kam doppelt. In einem die Prozedur grausam verzögernden Zeitlupentempo. Gezielt und genüßlich. Der gepeinigte Mann mußte laut zählen. Er zählte bis 20. Dann hörte er auf. Der Schmerz verschlug ihm die Stimme. Die SS-Leute hieben ungerührt weiter mit aller Wucht auf ihn ein. Mit roten Köpfen und hart aus dem Oberarm tretenden Muskeln.[168]

Leopold Figl, who in 1945 was to become the first Federal Chancellor of the post-war Second Republic, was given far worse treatment in a death cell, where he was fed only every third day, because he had been overheard using the term "Österreich" instead of "Ostmark" in a private conversation:

Ein paar Wochen später war Figl daran. Er hatte während der Freizeit vor der Baracke mit einem Kameraden geplaudert. Ein auf seinem Fahrrad unvermutet anpreschender Scharführer faßte ihn an der Brust.
"Schutzgefangener Leopold Figl meldet sich beim Herrn Unterscharführer gehorsamst zur Stelle".
"Wovon habt ihr eben gesprochen?"

"Melde gehorsamst, wir haben nur von zu Hause gesprochen".
"Wo bist du zu Hause?"
"In Österreich".
"Und mich anlügen auch noch! In der Ostmark bist du zu Hause. Marsch ab in den Bunker, wo man es dir beibringen wird, du dämlicher Hund!" Vor dem Radfahrer herlaufend, landete Figl im Lagerarrest, dem Zellentrakt für die Verdammten im Bunker. Sie ersparten es uns, seine Zerfleischung mitanzusehen, da, um die hektische Arbeit im Lageraufbau nicht zu unterbrechen, vorläufig kein offizieller "Schlageter", wie schwarzer Humor die sadistischen Orgien nannte, stattfinden sollte. Leopold Figl hatte seine Nerven in der Barbarei unseres von Tag zu Tag trostloser werdenden Alltags wiedergefunden. Er verbrachte, zuschanden geprügelt, sechs volle Wochen in einer Dunkelzelle, in einer Todeszelle, und bekam nach der menschenmordenden Vorschrift nur jeden dritten Tag etwas zu essen.[169]

The Nazis even made money out of their atrocities in Dachau. Gerda Hoffer wrote of a cousin of hers who was beaten to death in the camp, whereupon his wife and son were notified that they could collect his ashes for a large sum of money:

Der erste aus der Familie, der in ein Konzentrationslager geschickt wurde, war Leo Köhler. 70 Jahre vorher hatten seine Eltern ihren Namen Kahane in Köhler geändert, um nicht die antisemitischen Gefühle ihrer Nachbarn zu wecken. Die Enkel dieser Nachbarn zerrten nun Leo in ein altes, längst nicht mehr benutztes Schulgebäude, wo sie ihn stundenlang verprügelten, bevor er nach Dachau transportiert wurde. Einige Monate später erhielten seine Frau und sein Sohn die Mitteilung, er sei dort an einem Herzanfall gestorben und seine Asche könne gegen Bezahlung einer großen Summe abgeholt werden.[170]

The camp north-west of Munich began to take on a distinctly Austrian character in the course of the transportations that were to follow. Meanwhile, plans were initiated for an Austrian concentration camp at Mauthausen. In Gmunden the Gauleiter August Eigruber announced to a large crowd that Upper Austria had been singled out for a special distinction: "Nach Oberösterreich kommt das Konzentrationslager für die Volksverräter von ganz Österreich".[171] A roar of enthusiasm interrupted the speech. Mauthausen was soon to take over a system which had been well tried in Dachau: that of allowing "Aryan" prisoners doing sentences for violent crimes – so-called "Kapos", who, if anything, surpassed the SS in brutality – to oversee the Jewish inmates. Jakob Ehrlich, the former vice-president of the Jewish "Kultusgemeinde" in Vienna, was kicked to death in

Dachau in June 1938. The popular cabaret artist Fritz Grünbaum was also among those who were murdered. The brilliant young playwright and cabaret writer Jura Soyfer, who had been arrested on the very first day of the Anschluss, 13 March, while trying to ski over the Austrian-Swiss border, was transported from Vienna to Dachau in June 1938. While there, Soyfer wrote his "Dachau-Lied" in the style of ballads of workers' struggle, transforming the cynical motto over the gates of the concentration camp, "Arbeit macht frei", into a slogan of resistance. The song must have had a very uplifting effect, being passed secretly around the camp and learnt off by heart by the inmates. But in view of the long period of time for which Dachau would continue to do its deadly work and the end which Soyfer himself met, the optimistic refrain strikes a leaden note. He was transported to Buchenwald, where he was confined at night in overcrowded barracks without toilets. As a direct consequence of the intentionally unhygienic conditions there, he contracted typhus and died in a Weimar hospital on 16 February 1939 at the age of 27. An exit permit had been obtained and his release approved only a few days before:

Stacheldraht, mit Tod geladen,
Ist um unsre Welt gespannt.
Drauf ein Himmel ohne Gnaden
Sendet Frost und Sonnenbrand.
Fern von uns sind alle Freuden,
Fern die Heimat und die Fraun,
Wenn wir stumm zur Arbeit schreiten,
Tausende im Morgengraun.

Doch wir haben die Losung von Dachau gelernt
Und wir wurden stahlhart dabei.
Bleib ein Mensch, Kamerad,
Sei ein Mann, Kamerad,
Mach ganze Arbeit, pack an, Kamerad:
Denn Arbeit, denn Arbeit macht frei,
Denn Arbeit, denn Arbeit macht frei!

Vor der Mündung der Gewehre
Leben wir bei Tag und Nacht.
Leben wird uns hier zur Lehre,
Schwerer, als wir's je gedacht.
Keiner mehr zählt Tag und Wochen,
Mancher schon die Jahre nicht.
Und so viele sind zerbrochen
Und verloren ihr Gesicht.

Doch wir haben die Losung von Dachau gelernt
Und wir wurden stahlhart dabei.
Bleib ein Mensch, Kamerad,
Sei ein Mann, Kamerad,
Mach ganze Arbeit, pack an, Kamerad:
Denn Arbeit, denn Arbeit macht frei,
Denn Arbeit, denn Arbeit macht frei!

Schlepp den Stein und zieh den Wagen,
Keine Last sei dir zu schwer.
Der du warst in fernen Tagen,
Bist du heut schon längst nicht mehr.
Stich den Spaten in die Erde,
Grab dein Mitleid tief hinein
Und im eignen Schweiße werde
Selber du zu Stahl und Stein.

Doch wir haben die Losung von Dachau gelernt
Und wir wurden stahlhart dabei.
Bleib ein Mensch, Kamerad,
Sei ein Mann, Kamerad,
Mach ganze Arbeit, pack an, Kamerad:
Denn Arbeit, denn Arbeit macht frei,
Denn Arbeit, denn Arbeit macht frei!

Einst wird die Sirene künden:
Auf zum letzten Zählappell!
Draußen dann, wo wir uns finden,
Bist du, Kamerad, zur Stell.
Hell wird uns die Freiheit lachen,
Vorwärts geht's mit frischem Mut
Und die Arbeit, die wir machen,
Diese Arbeit, die wird gut!

Doch wir haben die Losung von Dachau gelernt
Und wir wurden stahlhart dabei.
Bleib ein Mensch, Kamerad,
Sei ein Mann, Kamerad,
Mach ganze Arbeit, pack an, Kamerad:
Denn Arbeit, denn Arbeit macht frei,
Denn Arbeit, denn Arbeit macht frei![172]

The authors, or even the distributors of such broadsheet texts, if found out, received the death penalty, as in the case of the Viennese nun Helene Kafka. A shoemaker's daughter and member of the Franciscan Order (officially called Sister Restituta but nicknamed Sister Resoluta due to her no-nonsense personality), an imperious but big-hearted nun, a popular and dedicated nurse and a robust, worldy-wise woman who preferred to drink her beer from the bottle, she drew unfavourable attention upon herself in the Mödling Hospital where she worked as an operating theatre sister by re-hanging crucifixes on the ward walls after they had been removed by order of the Nazi regime. She was openly rebellious against a National Socialist Dr Stumfohl who wanted to do away with the Last Rites in the hospital. She drew his wrath upon herself by bringing the crucifix to those dying patients who wanted religious solace in their last hours. When she was spied upon while asking a sister in the X-ray department to type out a hand-written text and make stencil copies of it, her fate was sealed. A befriended nun of the Congregation of Good Shepherds, Sister Agnes, recalled the day:

> als mir Sr. Restituta mit innerer Erregung, aber ohne Angst anvertraute, daß sie ein Spottgedicht auf Hitler in die Maschine diktiert habe und, da die Türe nicht ganz geschlossen gewesen sei, abgehört worden sei.

> Sr. Restituta sagte dann mit Zuversicht: "Es sind nun 14 Tage vorbei, so wird es keine Folgen haben".[173]

It can be deduced with some certainty from these words that Helena Kafka wrote the text herself, presumably with the intention of passing it on to soldier acquaintances or patients in the hospital. Whether it was her work or not, she obviously identified with it. The text bears the stamp of the amateur balladeer, with its clumsy rhythms and inconsistent metre and rhyming scheme, but is nonetheless of extraordinary documentary and human interest in corroborating and appealing to the growing conviction among the Austrian soldiers absorbed into the Wehrmacht that they were being sent to the front as cannon fodder before their German fellow-soldiers and that Austria had been annexed purely for military reasons rather than those of pan-Germanic fraternity. Among Austrian soldiers returning from the war front one heard more and more frequently the sentiment being expressed: "Die Ostmärker schickt man nach vorn, nur zum Erschießen; die Norddeutschen bleiben hinten".[174] It is obvious, therefore, that the poem, if Helene Kafka had managed to pass it on, would have fallen on fertile ground. It also demonstrates a greater degree of political discernment on the part of the so-called "common people" than had been evident at the time of the Anschluss among the Austrian bourgeoisie:

> Erwacht Soldaten und seid bereit,
> Gedenkt Eures ersten Eids für das Land,
> in dem Ihr gelebt und geboren,
> für Österreich habt ihr alle geschworen.
> Das sieht ja schon heute jedes Kind,

daß wir von den Preußen verraten sind.
Für die uralte heimische Tradition,
haben sie nichts als Spott und Hohn.
Den altösterreichischen General
kommandiert ein Gefreiter von dazumal.
Und der östreichische Rekrut
ist für sie nur als Kanonenfutter gut.
Zum Beschimpfen und Leuteschinden
mögen sie andere Opfer finden.
Mit ihrem großen preußischen Maul
sind sie uns herabzusetzen nicht faul.
Dafür haben sie bis auf den letzten Rest
die Ostmarkzitrone ausgepreßt.
Unser Gold und Kunstschätze schleppten sie gleich
in ihr abgewirtschaftetes Nazireich.
Unser Fleisch, Obst, Milch und Butter
waren für sie ein willkommenes Futter.
Sie befreiten uns und ehe mans glaubt
hatten sie uns gänzlich ausgeraubt.
Selbst den ruhmvollen Namen stahl sie uns die Brut
und jetzt wollen sie auch noch unser Blut.
Der Bruder Schnürschuh ist nicht dumm,
geb acht, er dreht die Gewehre um.
Der Tag der Vergeltung ist nicht mehr weit,
Soldaten gedenkt eures ersten Eids.
Österreich!
Wir Österreicher auf uns gestellt,
hatten Frieden und Freundschaft mit aller Welt.
Die Welt vergiftet mit ihrem Haß
Sie macht sich jedes Volk zum Feind.
Sie haben die Welt gegen sich vereint.
Die Mütter zittern, die Männer bangen,
der Himmel ist schwarz mit Wolken behangen.
Der schrecklichste Krieg, den der Menschheit gekannt,
steht furchtbar vor unserem Heimatland.
Es droht uns Elend und Hungersnot,
der Männer und Jünglinge Massentod,
Kameraden trotz dem verderblichen Wahn,
was gehen uns die Händel der Preußen an?
Was haben uns die Völker getan?
Wir nehmen die Waffen nur in die Hand
Im Kampf fürs freie Vaterland![175]

The poem is highly subversive in the given historical context, not only because it calls out the suppressed codeword "Österreich" and, worse still, refers to the "Führer" debunkingly as a mere "private from whenever-it-was" (surely as blasphemous as Bertolt Brecht's repeated use in his poems of the epithet "Anstreicher") but also because it is in so many ways true. The lines "Unser Gold und Kunstschätze schleppten sie gleich / in ihr abgewirtschaftetes Nazireich" exposes something which happened already in the very first days of the Anschluss. Already before 13 March an article had appeared in a German military gazette making Nazi intentions perfectly clear. Lili Körber commented:

> Darin wird von unserer Heimat wie von einem Gebrauchsgegenstand gesprochen. Hier gibt es keine Phrasen mehr von Rasse und deutschem Blut, sondern nur eine Aufzählung unserer Reichtümer, unseres Erdöls und Erdgases, unserer Wasserkräfte, unseres Fleisches und Fettes. Es ist die Rede von Blei, Zink, Kupfer, Graphit, Mangan und dem besonders wichtigen Magnesit, von den stillgelegten Goldbergwerken in den Hohen Tauern, die wieder in Betrieb gesetzt werden könnten, von den herrlichen Wäldern und der Nähe der beiden Rohstoffländer Jugoslawien und Ungarn, die besonders im Falle eines Krieges von einem nicht zu unterschätzenden Wert wären. Auch die Donau wird im Zusammenhang mit der Reichskriegsflotte erwähnt. Nein, das war kein "Anschluß", wir sind nicht Gleichberechtigte, sondern ein Kolonialvolk, das sich von dem Sieger ausplündern lassen muß![176]

Two days after the Heldenplatz speech, the considerable gold and foreign currency reserves of the Austrian National Bank amounting to 600 million Schilling were loaded onto a train to Berlin. A currency reform with an exchange rate of 1 Reichsmark to 1.5 Schilling paved the way to a systematic German buying up of Austrian production plants and shares. By 1943, Austrian share capital in the largest Austrian industries sank to 3.2% compared to 75.7% German capital. By 1944 the Germans owned 83% of Austrian banking, 70% of the mining and chemical industries, 60% of the engineering industry and 50% of building and transport. Many of the great works of art in Vienna became part of Göring's private collection. But it was an act of sedition to draw attention to these glaring facts. Dr Stumfohl reported Helene Kafka to the authorities, and on Ash Wednesday, 18 February, 1942, two Gestapo men walked straight into the operating theatre of Mödling Hospital and wanted to arrest her there and then. The operating surgeon protested because he needed her assistance throughout the operation, so they waited outside until it was completed. After several months' detention in the "Landesgericht Wien" she was sentenced to death for high treason on 29 October by the Nazi "Volksgericht", sent to the death cell for a further five months and, despite attempts by a prominent surgeon and a Mother Superior to intercede on her behalf (Cardinal Innitzer remaining silent), she was guillotined on 30 March, 1943. Martin Bormann had insisted on execution as a deterrent measure. With regard to the problem of how to deal with Helena Kafka's remains, the "Reichssicherheitshauptamt" expressed the following reservations:

> Hinsichtlich einer etwaigen Freigabe der Leiche der Kafka an deren Angehörige zur schlichten Bestattung hat die Staatspolizeileitstelle Wien insofern Bedenken, als dem Frauenorden, dem die Verurteilte angehört, die Rechte der Hinterbliebenen zukommen und von diesem Falle der Überlassung der Leiche eine unerwünschte Propaganda-tätigkeit und Verherrlichung der zum Tode Verurteilten als Märtyrerin zu erwarten ist.[177]

Only Nazis, like those so-called "Helden der Bewegung" who were executed for having had a part in the assassination of Dollfuß, could be celebrated as martyrs.

4.2 Harassment and flight

The pogroms of the euphemistically named "Kristallnacht" from 10–11 November, 1938, were reportedly more extreme in Austria than in Germany. All of Vienna's 4,038 Jewish shops had to close down and 1,950 Jewish homes were expropriated. Wilhelm R. Wagner summarizes the general situation regarding Jews: "Nach der 'Reichskristallnacht' ist der Verbleib für Juden im Deutschen Reich zur Überlebensfrage geworden; viele fliehen ins Ausland".[178] In their everyday lives, Franz Kafka's haunted vision of being subjected to a labyrinthine and inscrutable machinery of power was manifesting itself, as conveyed in the ironically titled poem "Das anständige Leben" by Berthold Viertel:

> Das anständige Leben ist es heute,
> Im Gefängnis verwahrt zu sein;
> Im Konzentrationslager eingesammelt;
> In der Folterkammer verköstigt;
> Oder auf der Flucht begriffen;
> Herumirrend an versperrten Grenzen;
> Vor Konsulaten wartend, im knauserigen Paßamt;
> Auf schwielenbildenden Bänken in Hilfsvereinen hockend,
> Ein Bettler, dem schlecht geholfen wird;
> Zu den Vertriebenen zu gehören, den umher Gejagten,
> Welche sie überall einsperren,
> Gegen die überall Krieg geführt wird,
> Von Freund und Feind, weil sie die Schwächeren sind;
> Ein Jude zu sein, den jeder mit einem Hintergedanken
>   anblickt;
> Ein Anwalt des arbeitenden Volkes,

Der keine Stelle mehr findet:
So sieht heute das anständige Leben aus,
Und es ist leicht zu haben.
Aber keiner begehrt es.[179]

In his novel fragment *Mainacht in Wien*, Leo Perutz describes the bureaucratic harassment that faced Jews who attempted to emigrate:

> Die Ausreiseerlaubnis wurde jedem zugesichert, der "politisch unbedenklich" war und sich der Zustimmung der Steuerbehörde vergewissert hatte.
>
> Die Steuerbehörde – das war aber nicht etwa ein einziges Amt, das seine Zustimmung erteilte oder verweigerte, sondern ein kompliziertes Gebilde aus den verschiedenartigsten, örtlich meist weit auseinanderliegenden Amtsstellen, deren jede sich mit einer anderen Steuerquelle zu befassen hatte. Deren gab es viele. Man hatte nachzuweisen, daß man die Erwerbs-, die Umsatz- und die Rentensteuer pünktlich entrichtet hatte, daß man an Erbschafts-, Krisen- und Hundesteuer keinen Pfennig schuldete, mit der Wohnbau-, der Mietaufwand- und der Zinsgroschensteuer nicht im Rückstand war und daß man auch hinsichtlich aller anderen Abgaben und Gebühren ein reines Gewissen besaß. Ämter [...] traten aus dem Dunkel ihrer Verborgenheit hervor, machten ihre Forderungen geltend und wollten befriedigt oder wenigstens beachtet und befragt werden.[180]

There is a similar passage in George Clare's *Last Waltz in Vienna*:

> The proverbial Austrian sloth was now transformed into state policy and used to harass and offend the Jewish petitioner. Surprises awaited one at every office when, after queueing for hours at the still constant risk of being hijacked from the queue by a passing S.A. or S.S. patrol for a few hours of cleaning their barracks, one finally faced the official one had come to see. In eight cases out of ten one learned then that one had done it all wrong. Back to the starting point and get a chit to another office to get a chit from another official entitling one to talk to the first one. And when one had come back, duly equipped with the required piece of paper, after queueing for another few hours, needless to say, then this stamp was not right or that document wrong and one started all over again. The inventiveness of the Nazi officials knew no bounds.[181]

Lilian R. Furst summarizes the intractable situation in which Jews found themselves:

> Paradoxically, the Nazis wanted to be rid of the Jews, yet invented innumerable obstacles to emigration. You had to

have not only a current passport, but also certificates that your rent, gas, electricity, telephone, and taxes were fully paid, that you were not abandoning any property, and that you didn't have a relative in an insane asylum as a burden to the state. Each of these certificates was valid for only one month, so that it was virtually impossible to get them all together at the same time. Hardest of all to obtain was a visa to another country; no one wanted us.[182]

The increasing reluctance of foreign countries to take on German and Austrian Jews compounded the already enormous problems. Czechoslovakia and Hungary had closed their borders on the first day of the Anschluss – Jewish families or antifascists who travelled to the borders in the hope of escape were simply placed on a non-stop train back to Vienna. Robert Breuer describes the scenes at the Austrian-Hungarian border on the first day of the Anschluss:

An der österreichischen Grenzstation flatterte bereits die Hakenkreuzfahne, die Formalitäten wurden rasch erledigt – voll Hoffnung fuhren die Leute zur ungarischen Grenzstation. Wie furchtbar war ihre Enttäuschung, als alle in Hegyeshalom zum Verlassen des Zuges aufgefordert wurden und zu hören bekamen: "Der Retour-Zug nach Wien steht bereits bereit!" Nur Passagieren mit ungarischen Pässen war der Grenzübertritt gestattet. Männer tobten und weinten wie kleine Kinder, Frauen baten und flehten in Schrei- und Weinkrämpfen, Kinder weinten und schluchzten – aber die Organe des "Nachbarlandes" blieben all diesen Bitten gegenüber taub. Alle Menschlichkeit versagte – wie so oft in jenen Tagen – vor der unverständlichen Strenge der Gesetze und Verfügungen. Schließlich blieb den Verzweifelten, die Österreichs Grenze bereits hinter sich hatten, nichts übrig, als den bitterkalten "Retourzug" zu besteigen und die Heimfahrt anzutreten. Mit einem "Aha, da ist er ja wieder, der Judenzug!" wurden die Leute wieder auf österreichischem Boden empfangen. In dem Stück Land zwischen den Grenzstationen stand österreichisches Militär, bis an die Zähne bewaffnet, so daß keinem der Zuginsassen möglich war, "abzuspringen" und – ohne Ballast von Gepäck – in die ersehnte Freiheit zu laufen ...[183]

The Klaar family's attempt to obtain a visa to Britain was thwarted by a vote in the House of Commons on 22 March, 1938, not to give the Home Office emergency powers to admit more Austrian refugees. Georg Klaar, who was later to change his name to George Clare, commented bitterly:

After that vote Sir Samuel Hoare, the Home Secretary, explained that he would examine carefully and sym-pathetically applications from Austrian refugees working in science, the arts, business and industry, whose presence in the country may be advantageous to Britain. In less elegant words his message was: If you are just a Jew fleeing from Nazi persecution, keep out. If, by wealth or training you are a person useful to us, then you might come in, even if you are a Jew.

Britain, of course, was by no means the only country to react like this. Within a few hours of the *Anschluß* Czechoslovakia, long hailed as the only true democracy and the most liberal state in Central Europe, sealed its borders against Jewish refugees from Austria. Paul-Henri Spaak, the Belgian politician, reputed to be one of Europe's foremost liberal statesmen, announced in his parliament that there could be no "wholesale" admission of foreigners into his country. And the U.S. Secretary of State, Cordell Hull, while proposing the setting up of a special international committee for political refugees, made it quite clear that no increase in the German and Austrian immigration quotas could be contemplated. Europe's oldest popular democracy, Switzerland, became so worried about the influx of Jews from Greater Germany that her police chief Dr Heinrich Rothmund, not Hitler's S.S., had his name recorded by history as the originator of the large red "J" stamped on the passports of the Reich's Jewish second-class citizens. He justified this step with the excuse that as there were no visas required for Germans entering Switzerland, and vice versa, his border policemen often could not tell Jewish from "Aryan" Germans.[184]

The Klaars were later to have severe trouble in obtaining visas for the Irish Free State and, even after they had been granted by an Irish administration reluctant to allow entry to any Jews that had not converted to Catholicism, they were confronted with obstructions on the part of the Irish Ambassador in Berlin, Charles Bewley, an anti-Semite and enthusiastic admirer of the Hitler Regime. In all, Ireland issued visas to hardly more than 60 Jewish refugees between 1939 and 1945. S. A. Roche, the then secretary of the Department of Justice, summed up in 1946 the Irish wartime "aliens" policy, still indulging in the very stereotypes that had made the Holocaust possible in the first place:

> Our practice has been to discourage any substantial increase in the Jewish population. They do not assimilate with our own people but remain a sort of colony of a world-wide Jewish community. This makes them a potential irritant in the body politic and has led to disastrous results from time to time in other countries.[185]

Hubert Butler wrote of Ireland at the time of the Anschluss:

> The mood in Ireland was one of ignorant indifference. It was expressed in the Dáil in 1943 by a very pious Catholic, Oliver Flanagan. "There is one thing," he said, "that the Germans did and that was to rout the Jews out of their country". He added that we should rout them out of Ireland: "They crucified our Saviour 1,900 years ago and they have been crucifying us every day of the week". No one contradicted him.[186]

Butler himself went to Vienna in 1938 and '39 to help the Quakers in the *Freundeszentrum* in the Singerstrasse to mediate for Jews seeking visas.

The hard pressed Jews of Austria were let know what the rest of the world thought of them by the World Refugee Conference held in Evian-les-Bains on Lake Geneva in July, 1938. George Clare writes:

> There was not a Jew under German dominion who did not look towards that spa with hopeful expectations. The representatives of thirty-two countries assembled there, listened to evidence, conferred and deliberated, talked and considered: and, after a few weeks at Evian, came to the conclusion that they could not – oh, so regrettably – find a place for the Jews anywhere in the world, not even for their children.[187]

The Irishman Hubert Butler was sent by the *Freundeszentrum* as their representative to the Evian conference:

> I talked to two delegates from Ireland, or rather from the Irish embassies in Paris and Berne. One remarked, "Didn't we suffer like this in the Penal Days and nobody came to our help".

> When I got back [to Vienna] I visited all the embassies to get visas for the emigrating Jews. There was a kindly official at the Mexican embassy who would sign an entry visa for anyone who asked. Even though it might fail to get them into Mexico it would get them out of Austria. So many applicants arrived that he had to get his wife and family in to help him.[188]

That was very much a laudable and otherwise unsung exception to the rule. Stefan Zweig quotes a Russian exile as saying: "Früher hatte der Mensch nur einen Körper und eine Seele. Heute braucht man noch einen Paß dazu, sonst wird er nicht wie ein Mensch behandelt".[189] Describing his own experiences in attempting to enter Britain, Zweig wrote:

All die Erniedrigungen, die man früher ausschließlich für Verbrecher erfunden hatte, wurden jetzt vor und während der Reise jedem Reisenden auferlegt. Man mußte sich photographieren lassen von rechts und links, im Profil und en face, das Haar so kurz geschnitten, daß man das Ohr sehen konnte, man mußte Fingerabdrücke geben, erst nur den Daumen, dann alle zehn Finger, mußte überdies Zeugnisse, Gesundheitszeugnisse, Impfzeugnisse, polizeiliche Führungs-zeugnisse, Empfehlungen vorweisen, mußte Einladungen präsentieren können und Adressen von Verwandten, mußte moralische und finanzielle Garantien beibringen, Formulare ausfüllen und unterschreiben in dreifacher, vierfacher Ausfertigung, und wenn nur eines aus diesem Schock Blätter fehlte, war man verloren.[190]

In the case of Theodor Kramer, who applied for an immigration visa to the United States, he was told to supply affidavits and declarations of earnings from three American citizens. Having sought out distant relatives in America who did supply the required certificates of support, he was told that the affidavits were incomplete and that one of the citizens, a Mrs Hila Crayder Meadow whom Kramer had never met, would have to forward a declaration of intent to supply Kramer with a dwelling as well as $15 per week for his keep, an estimation of the value of her jewellery authenticated by a notary, a declaration of the value of her separated husband's property, his tax statements from the previous two years, his bank account statements and a declaration of earnings from his employers. The good woman actually supplied all of these documents in the realization of Kramer's life-and-death predicament, upon which the American Consulate discovered further inadequacies in all three affidavits. The entire procedure, which had taken exactly a year, was in vain. He then applied to the Police Department of St. Gallen for the right to cross the border into Switzerland and received the answer: "Die Grenze ist seit Samstag für Emigranten jeder Art vollständig gesperrt. Es ist unmöglich, Ihrem Wunsche zu entsprechen".[191] Ironically, the franking bore the motto "Ferien in der Schweiz". Kramer then applied for a visa at the Swiss Embassy. The Police Department in Berne first demanded from him a fee of Mk 15, – "zur Deckung der Kosten, für die Sie im Falle der Abweisung aufzukommen haben", and, after receiving the fee, rejected his application on the grounds that there was no guarantee that he would leave Switzerland immediately: "Die Weiterreise ist nicht gesichert".[192]

He then applied to Britain – relatively speaking, the most accessible, or rather, the least inaccessible country in the non-occupied parts of Europe – for a permit to work alongside his wife Rosa, who had already fled and was working as domestic servant in a house near Wolverhampton. (Under public pressure the Tory government had issued immigration permits after the "Kristallnacht" to Jewish children as well as to Jewish women willing to work as housemaids. Men who guaranteed that they would leave Britain again were allowed to wait for their immigration papers in Camp Kitchener in Kent.) The lady of the house, a Mrs Willcock, agreed to employ Theodor Kramer, too, but the British Passport Control Officer in Vienna rejected his application because he was not convinced of Kramer's ability to carry out the functions of a domestic servant. Eventually, a letter on Kramer's behalf from Thomas Mann to the British Home Office was successful, but not before Kramer had attended a cookery course and supplied a certificate of good health. To satisfy the Austrian authorities he had to go through the same procedures as described above by Leo Perutz. On his way through Belgium in July 1939, the border guards there stamped into his passport that it was forbidden "de s'arrêter volontairement en Belgique ou de s'y établir".[193]

In the course of this prolonged ordeal, the constant and growing threat from the immediate social environment as well as the callousness of the foreign immigration authorities, the enforced evacuation of his flat in the Kaasgrabengasse, the move to his mother's cramped accommodation in the Goltzstraße, which in turn they were forced to vacate, and finally going into hiding in a tiny flat on the fifth floor of a house in the Lazarettgasse, Kramer suffered a nervous breakdown and was brought by friends for a short period of recuperation to a house in the Hameaustraße in Neustift im Walde. This is codified as "das grüne Haus" in the extraordinary volume of very realistic "Erlebnislyrik" written at the time, *Wien 1938*. The cycle of thirty-two poems, all the more troubling for being written in colloquial diction and conventional uniform quatrains of iambic pentameter, mostly with an a-b-a-b rhyme scheme and end-stop lines, are the attempts of a sensitive mind to ward off insanity by a form-creating discipline, "daß ich dem Nichts nur widerstehen kann, / wenn ich die Angst vor ihm in Verse bann".[194] They tell of the confinement in flats packed with furniture, the limited and senseless daily routine, the wary journeys to office after office, the disorientation caused by changing flats, the never-ending anxiety, the shock of waking up each day, the inordinate gratefulness for normal interactions with members of the non-Jewish population like the local grocer, the relief at having small repairs to carry out to fill the yawning emptiness, the listing of objects as guarantees of normality and anchorage in an effort to convince oneself of one's existence, the poet's physical and mental deterioration, as in the poem "Gegen Früh":

Tagsüber steht man um Papiere Schlange,
mit einem Pulver schläft man abends ein;
man träumt, doch richtig wird erst einem bange,
füllt gegen Früh das Zimmer fahler Schein.

Verkrustet heben sich die schweren Lider,
man liegt ganz zugedeckt als wie im Wind;
in ihren Beugen regen sich die Glieder
und wissen plötzlich wieder, wo sie sind.

Der Kopf beginnt darüber nachzusinnen,
was noch bevorsteht und was niemand weiß,
und tausend Dingen kann man nicht entrinnen,
und die Gedanken gehn verstört im Kreis.

Dann ist es gut, schon vorgemerkt zu finden:
heut ist auf dies und jenes Amt zu gehn,
ein Draht ist ums gesprungne Schaff zu binden,
ein Futter für den Mantel zu erstehn.

Die Crême verreibt sich in die trocknen Hände,
und langsam wird man der Verwirrung Herr;
schon dringt des Nachbars Prusten durch die Wände,
und rings beginnt das Radio sein Geplärr,

der Rock hängt auf dem Bügel in der Helle.
Wie ist doch auf die Dinge noch Verlaß!
Die Viertelflasche Milch steht vor der Schwelle,
darüber werden jäh die Augen naß.[195]

Despite the outstanding quality of *Wien 1938*, the poem "Die Wahrheit ist, man hat mir nichts getan" is the only one of the cycle to have achieved anthology status:

Die Wahrheit ist, man hat mir nichts getan.
Ich darf schon lang in keiner Zeitung schreiben,
die Mutter darf noch in der Wohnung bleiben.
Die Wahrheit ist, man hat mir nichts getan.

Der Greisler schneidet mir den Schinken an
und dankt mir, wenn ich ihn bezahle, kindlich;
wovon ich leben werd, ist unerfindlich.
Die Wahrheit ist, man hat mir nichts getan.

Ich fahr wie früher mit der Straßenbahn
und gehe unbehelligt durch die Gassen;

ich weiß bloß nicht, ob sie mich gehen lassen.
Die Wahrheit ist, man hat mir nichts getan.

Es öffnet sich mir in kein Land die Bahn,
ich kann mich nicht von selbst von hinnen heben:
ich habe einfach keinen Raum zum Leben.
Die Wahrheit ist, man hat mir nichts getan.[196]

The first line returns four times, as if the poet were trying to persuade himself that conditions are actually normal, or at least acceptable. The rest of the poem divides into a corroboration of normality (lines 3, 5–6, 9–10) and a denial of it (lines 2, 7, 11, 13–15), the latter gaining the upper hand and thus ultimately belying the anxiously repeated self-reassurance that all is well. But even the lines which want to present the situation as normal raise the question about the nature of a "normal" situation in which an ageing mother has to be *allowed* to remain in her flat. How could it be that a citizen might *not* be able to ride in the tram or go unmolested through the streets? Oppressive measures, however cruel they may be, if introduced gradually and couched in legalistic jargon, have the effect that even the victims try to accommodate them. The poem thematizes the victim's internalization of the prevailing ideology as well as conveying in the self-contradictory nature of the text the pathological effects of such victimization and internalization.

Before the Wannsee Conference, Adolf Eichmann, officially titled "Expert in Jewish Matters", had relentlessly carried out his task of driving as many Jews out of Austria as possible – 126,000 from Vienna alone – after first systematically robbing them of their property and assets. But even previous to the "Endlösung" being made policy, he and his office dedicated themselves from October 1939 on with equal alacrity to *preventing* Jews from leaving Austria so that they could be deported to ghettos and camps in Poland. Transportations were now becoming part of everyday life. The 18-year-old Erwin Chvojka wrote this poem in balladic style in 1942 as an eye-witness record of what was happening:

Der Judenzug

Am Schwedenplatz die Uhr zeigt zwei,
da gehts in rascher Fahrt vorbei.

In den wirbelnden Staub der Straße gehüllt
zwei graue Wagen mit Menschen gefüllt.

Auf Kisten und Ballen zusammengepreßt
ein Judenzug die Stadt verläßt.

Sie sitzen und liegen, gedrückt und verzagt,
zerbrochne Gestalten vom Schicksal gejagt.

Ein Junge nur aufrecht im Wagen steht
und trotzig sein Haar im Winde weht.

Die Alten hocken mit stumpfem Sinn
und starrn in die Ferne: wohin – wohin?[197]

Under the supervision of the former Gauleiter of Vienna, Odilo Globocnik, one third of Austria's 220,000 Jewish citizens were brought to their death in this way, to Lodz, Riga, Minsk, Chelmno, Lublin, Auschwitz. Theodor Kramer escaped in time. Kramer's mother, Rosa, who chose to stay on in her native city, was ultimately transported to Theresienstadt. From London Erich Fried was able to arrange for a British visa to be issued to his mother Nelly and so rescued her, but his beloved grandmother, Malvine Stein, who remained in Vienna, was first transported to Theresienstadt and then, at the age of 79, to the gas chambers of Auschwitz.

5. The "Final Solution"

The brilliant Viennese sociologist, Dr Käthe Leichter, who had campaigned all her life for the rights of working women and particularly of the most exploited group of all, housemaids, had already been harassed by the Dollfuß-Schuschnigg Austro-fascist regime as a prominent member and ideologue of the Revolutionary Socialists. After the Annexation, the files of the "Fatherland Front" secret police fell into the hands of the National Socialists, who stepped up the persecution against leftist activists, particularly when, as in the case of Käthe Leichter, they were Jewish as well. While her husband Otto and her two young sons, Heinz and Franzl, escaped to freedom, she stayed on in Vienna because of her ailing mother. In April 1938 she was supplied with a forged passport and a visa to Czechoslovakia and made preparations to flee. Unknown to her, one of her fellow-members of the Revolutionary Socialists, Hans Pav, acted as an informer to the Gestapo on her every move. Before leaving for the train to the Czech border, she rang her mother once more to take leave of her. Instead of her mother, a Gestapo agent answered the phone and said to her: "Wir wissen, wo Sie sind, kommen Sie sofort her, sonst werden Sie Ihre Mutter nie wieder sehen".[198] She was arrested "wegen Verdachtes des Verbrechens der Vorbereitung zum Hochverrat gem. §83 Abs. 2, §80 Abs. 2 RSTG im Sinne des §112 RSTPO",[199] to quote the chilling pseudo-officialese of the Volksgericht, and was incarcerated in the Landesgericht in Vienna. Her mother threw herself out of a fourth-storey window. On 13 October 1939, a Belgian visa was issued for Käthe Leichter, but instead of being freed and let rejoin her family she was transported in January 1940 to the women's concentration camp at Ravensbrück, north of Berlin. There she was forced to carry out heavy road-building work and the loading of bricks onto ships on the Havel river, so that her hands were bloodied and festering. She took to secretly writing poetry as a means of maintaining her sense of optimism. The poem *An meine Brüder* has the life-affirmative and defiant tone of socialist songs. It came down to posterity by being learnt off by heart by a young Communist woman who was to survive the camp:

Bruder, schreckst auch du des Nachts empor aus wirren
   Träumen,
sind es Bilder, tags bewußt, die nachts den Schlaf
   umsäumen?
Warst du heute nacht bei Weib und Kind?
Ich war bei meinen Kindern. Deckte beide zu und sprach:
"Mutter kommt bald, brav sein und nicht weinen!"
Die Lampe warf ihr Licht auf Buch und Sofaecke,
wir saßen still, mein Mann und ich, daß nichts die Kinder
   wecke.
Da schreckt' ich auf. Fahl schien der Mond auf eiserne
   Gestelle.
Und da lieg ich unter vielen und doch so einsam und so kalt.
Ich in Ravensbrück, du in Sachsenhausen, in Dachau oder in
   Buchenwald.

Bruder, stehst du des Morgens frierend beim Appell?
Wir stehen stumm in Zehnerreihen, im Osten wird es
   langsam hell.
Steil ragt der Wald, wir atmen Luft in vollen Zügen,
Kräfte zu sammeln für den schweren Tag,
denn keiner von uns darf, will je unterliegen.
Da flammt's im Osten seltsam auf, als stünde die Welt in
   Flammen.
Wir nehmen's als gutes Zeichen. Bricht wirklich bald alles
   zusammen?
Und dann stehen wir stumm, nur die Fäuste geballt,
ich in Ravensbrück, du in Sachsenhausen, in Dachau oder in
   Buchenwald.

Bruder, stehst du auch des Tags mit der Schaufel in der
   Hand,
wird es nicht Mittag? Nimmt denn kein End' der Sand?
Oder schleppst auch du wie ich große schwere Steine?
Schmerzt auch dich der Rücken, brennen die Beine?
Sieh, du bist doch ein Mann, gewohnt an's harte Schlagen,
ich bin schwächer und mein Leib hat schon Kinder getragen.
Wie denkst du über unsrer Kinder Leben?
Werden Schläge, Strafblock, stets als Drohung schweben?
Und dann geht es weiter noch, im Herzen Hoffnung und Halt:
Ich in Ravensbrück, du in Sachsenhausen, in Dachau oder in
   Buchenwald.

Oh, Bruder, einmal kommt der Morgen, wo uns kein Appell
   mehr hält!
Wo weit offen die Tore, und vor uns liegt die große, die freie
   Welt.
Und dann werden wir KZler auf der breiten Straße wandern.
Doch auf uns warten noch die andern.
Und wer uns sieht, sieht die Furchen, die das Leid uns in das
   Antlitz geschrieben,
sieht Spuren von Körper- und Seelenqualen, die uns ein

bleibendes Mal geblieben.
Und wer uns sieht, sieht auch den Zorn, der hell in unseren
   Augen blitzt,
sieht den jauchzenden Freiheitsjubel, der ganz unsere Herzen
   besitzt.
Und dann reihen wir uns ein, in die letzte große Kolonne,
dann heißt es zum letzten Male: Vorwärts, marsch!
Und jetzt führt der Weg zum Licht und zur Sonne.
Oh, Bruder, siehst du gleich mir diesen Tag, du mußt doch
   denken: Er kommt bald!
Und dann ziehen wir aus Ravensbrück, aus Sachsenhausen,
   aus Dachau und aus Buchenwald.[200]

Soon, the sordid reality of Nazism was to break relentlessly
upon her. In February 1942 Käthe Leichter, along with 1,500
other Jewish women, was transported from the Ravensbrück
camp in a cattle wagon to a "trial" gassing in anticipation of
the mass extermination camps of Auschwitz and Treblinka.
Her friend Gabriele Proft described the funeral in Vienna and
the inconceivable cynicism of the Nazi authorities in
informing the relatives that Käthe had passed away at 3
o'clock and in sending them a bill for the delivery of the
ashes:

Da kam die Nachricht, daß Käthe am 17. März 1942 in
Ravensbrück gestorben sei. Ob man die Urne wünsche? Die
Urne kam und mit ihr der letzte Brief ihrer Kinder, der sie
nicht mehr erreicht hatte. Man gab ihn ihr mit in den Sarg.
Am 24. April 1942 um 12 Uhr 30 versammelten sich die
wenigen Freunde, die noch in Wien waren, um von einer
klugen Frau, einer gütigen Gattin und Mutter, einer tapferen
Sozialistin, Abschied zu nehmen. Da war auch eine kleine,
zarte Frau mit großen, todtraurigen Augen. Es war Ottos
Mutter, die an diesem gräßlichen Abschluß eines glücklichen
Ehelebens teilnahm. Ihr eigener Mann lag krank zu Hause.
Ob sich wohl heute noch jemand vorstellen kann, was es
heißt, mit schmerzerfülltem Herzen Abschied zu nehmen von
einem unschuldigen Menschen, der nie etwas anderes wollte,
als helfen. Dazustehen unter Menschen, von denen die
meisten wußten, daß Käthes Schicksal auch das ihre sein
wird. Alle zusammen in der Erwartung, verhaftet zu werden,
weil man an einem jüdischen Begräbnis teilgenommen hatte:
Im Gedenken an Otto und die Kinder, denen die Flucht ins
Ausland gelungen war, aber Gattin und Mutter auf so
grauenhafte Weise verloren hatten. Die Barbaren hatten
ihnen "zum Trost" sogar mitgeteilt, daß Käthe Leichter um
drei Uhr gestorben sei. Und eine Rechnung dazu geschickt.
"Ward je in solcher Laun' ein Mensch gemordet?" könnte man
mit Shakespeare sagen. Ins Ausland durften wir nur
schreiben, daß Käthe jetzt beim letzten Tor wohnt.[201]

The Jewish writer Mimi Großberg escaped in time to America, where she settled for the rest of her life. She returned in 1957 on a visit to her native Vienna and travelled out to the leafy suburb Hohe Warte on the slopes overlooking the city and the sweep of the Danube plain. She wanted to see what had become of a Jewish home for the blind in Hohe Warte which she had often visited before the Anschluss. The home was called "das Israelitische Blindeninstitut" and had an illustrious history. It is important to delve a little into that history just to see how social issues had been handled under the benign reign of Kaiser Franz Josef and before the advent of political anti-Semitism in Austria. The Jewish blind asylum was the brainchild of a Jewish poet and historian, Dr Ludwig August Frankl, who inspired the philanthropist, Baron Moritz von Königswarter, to finance its construction, completed in 1870. (As a result of this and other similar initiatives on the part of Frankl, he was awarded the title of "Ritter von Hochwart".) In 1897 an extra storey was added on through the sponsorship of Baroness Clara von Hirsch-Gereuth. The "Blindeninstitut" was innovative in being Austria's first home of this kind to introduce handicraft courses for the visually impaired as a means of instilling in them a sense of their own worth and their membership of society at large.[202] Mimi Großberg's poem about this venerable institution begs the question of who really sees ("deuteten ins Licht") or does not see, or in other words, who are really more disabled, the physically or metaphorically blind:

> Steht es auch noch, das große stille Haus?
> Was ist aus meinen Blinden nur geworden
> in all dem Hassen, Flüchten, Brennen, Morden?
> Ihrer gedenkend, fahr ich dort hinaus.
>
> Sie pflegten mir "den Blick" vom Dach des Heimes
> voll Stolz zu zeigen – deuteten ins Licht –
> aus toten Augen strahlten sie Geheimes,
> "besahen" mit den Fingern mein Gesicht.
>
> Da unten lag, betörend, sinnberauschend,
> die Stadt gebreitet und des Stromes Band,
> doch nicht für sie! und krampfhaft heiter plauschend,
> fuhr ich mir übers Auge mit der Hand.
>
> Noch steht es dort, das große stille Haus,
> hat überdauert Krieg und Nazihorden,
> Ein Polizeiamt wurde nun daraus.
> Doch: was ist aus den Blinden bloß geworden?[203]

The building serves as an unlikely looking police station to this day. Mimi Großberg's question about the whereabouts of the former occupants is, of course, rhetorical. On 6 August, 1941, a high-ranking military doctor took a name list of the inmates of the institute (some of whom had been blinded in fighting for Austria/Germany in the First World War) and left without a word of farewell. Soon afterwards, an order was issued that no inmates should be allowed to stroll past the nearby villa in which the new "Reichsstatthalter" Baldur von Schirach had taken up residence. One almost totally blind 75-year-old man, who strayed too far afield to a tobacco shop to buy cigarettes and was reported by the shopkeeper, was given a six-months house arrest. In the course of 1942, Hohe Warte, together with all other Jewish homes for the aged and infirm, hospitals and orphanages, was dissolved. The last forty blind were moved to three old age homes nearer the city centre and then transported in August 1942 to Theresienstadt, supposedly the model ghetto for the aged, for war-disabled and for ex-servicemen awarded medals for bravery, but in fact a transit point on the way to the extermination camps.

Stella Rotenberg, on summoning up the courage to revisit the city from which she had been forced to flee at the age of 23, and once again enter the house where she had grown up and from which her parents were transported in 1942, wrote this harrowing poem in 1976. It is in two parts. In the second part, she expresses her shock at the *sameness* of the building, as if even stones that had echoed screams of anguish of that kind would somehow have to have registered them. The seemingly harmless title reveals itself already in the sub-title as bitterly ironic:

Besuch im Heimatort

(im Haus aus dem man sie zum Sterben holte)

I.

Mutter höre mich!
Ich habe überlebt!
Dein Kind hat Satan überlebt!

Sieh mich heute
wie ich die lange Treppe hinunterschreite –
deinen letzten Gang.

Ich setze meinen Fuß
auf die Fließen im Flur,
in die Fährte deines Fußes,
ich suche, suche deine Spur ...

Das Tor steht offen
so wie es offen stand zu deinem Tod.

O Zeit die nichts vermag, o Not.
Wir müssen ewig trauern.

                II.

Die Steine stehen.

Die Steine stehen und sie fallen,
sie fallen nicht
unter dem Gericht
der Schreie, der Schreie.

Es stehen die Mauern
die die Schreie überdauern,
die Wände stehen und sie zeigen
keine Zeichen ...

Die Häuser stehen und sie brechen,
sie brechen nicht
auf beim Aufstieg der Schreie,
sie brechen nicht auf!

Sie stehen
als sei nichts geschehen.[204]

Another postwar visit is documented in Erich Fried's poem "Sommer der Verjährung", written in 1968 on the 30th anniversary of his father's violent death at the hands of his Nazi interrogators. The word "Verjährung" in the title is a reference to the fact that, though in Austrian law Nazi murders did not lapse in the 30th year after they had been committed, those that were redefined in court as "manslaughter" did. The perpetrator of Hugo Fried's murder was never brought to justice, but led a comfortable existence as a senior civil servant in Düsseldorf. The poet describes a ride on the tram out to the Zentralfriedhof, where his father lies buried, and the aural and visual impressions on the way. However, this "neutral" text of three stanzas is problematized by being interfered with by contrapuntal text particles in the fourth, seventh and ninth verse of each stanza. Fried added this explanatory note:

> Die kursiv gedruckten Worte sind Formulierungen, wie sie in der Nazizeit verwendet wurden und beziehen sich auf die Juden. Das "Vierte Tor" des Wiener Zentralfriedhofs führt zu jenem Teil des jüdischen Friedhofs, wo sich die Gräber befinden, bei denen keine Angehörigen mehr da sind, die sie pflegen würden.[205]

The graves are neglected because the mourners, too, have been at best exiled, at worst exterminated. The anti-Semitic particles keep erupting into the atmospheric vignette of Vienna, like a suppressed memory into the sanitized atmosphere of 1968:

Es hat geregnet
es ist wieder heiß
das staubige Pflaster
    sind schuld
der Liechtensteinstraße
trocknet
    sind unser Unglück
und riecht noch wie nach der Schule
    müssen vernichtet werden

Der Friedhof
am Vierten Tor
verwahrlost
    sind schuld
die Straßenbahn
scheppert und klirrt
    sind unser Unglück
zwischen Doppelfenstern auf Brücken
    müssen vernichtet werden

Im Abendwind
vom Ende der Straße
graublaue Hügel
    sind schuld
am anderen Ende
patinagrün die Kuppel
    sind unser Unglück
oder ein stumpfer Kirchturm
    müssen vernichtet werden[206]

6. Resistance and collaboration

6.1 Resistance

It is important to differentiate when discussing the fascistic and anti-Semitic inclinations of the Austrians in general and the Viennese in particular. Erich Fried, himself a victim of those inclinations, never allowed himself the luxury of a sweeping condemnation. As in Ruth Klüger's experience of help from a kindly cinema attendant in Hietzing, Fried as a 17-year-old also received moral support, however ineffectual it was, from an unexpected quarter. In the anecdote "Man zeigt auf mich", he tells of how he was standing in a queue to bring some clothing to his mother who was in custody under the charge of having plotted to smuggle Austrian currency out of the country:

> Ich erinnere mich noch genau, wie ich an einem regnerischen Tag vor dem Jugendgerichtsgebäude Schlange stand, um meiner verhafteten Mutter irgendwelche Kleidungsstücke zu bringen. Die Gefängnisse und Polizeistellen waren alle ständig überfüllt. So waren viele Frauen im Jugendgericht eingesperrt, besonders Untersuchungshäftlinge wie meine Mutter.

> Ich stand im Regen und wartete. Das war nicht ganz ungefährlich. Manchmal kam SA oder SS und griff sich einige Leute zum Reinigen der Aborte in ihren Kasernen heraus. Dabei wurde man gelegentlich mißhandelt, abgesehen von der Demütigung. Manchmal wurde den zu solcher Arbeit Gepreßten auch Lauge oder Säure in ihr Waschwasser geschüttet, so daß sie sich die Hände beschädigten. Eigentlich wußte man, daß jeden Augenblick etwas geschehen konnte.

> Ein Mann und eine Frau mittleren Alters sahen mich an. Sie trugen Lodenmäntel, auf dem Kragen vorne das Parteiabzeichen. Ja, kein Zweifel, sie sahen mich an. Mir war nicht wohl unter ihren Blicken. Sie zeigten auf mich und kamen auf *mich* zu. Ich beschloß, mir meine Angst nicht anmerken zu lassen.

> Vielleicht meinten sie doch nicht mich? Ich sah meine Nachbarn in der Schlange der Wartenden an, aber die trugen alle ihre kleinen gestanzten Hakenkreuze. Nur ich nicht. Das hatten die beiden offenbar gesehen, als sie auf mich zeigten.

Nun stand die Frau neben mir und sagte: "Kommen Sie einen Augenblick da heraus". Es klang gar nicht unfreundlich, aber das konnte nichts Gutes zu bedeuten haben. Vielleicht gehörten sie zur Geheimen Staatspolizei, zur Gestapo? Die anderen in der Schlange taten, als sähen sie mich nicht.

Ich trat aus der Schlange heraus und ging mit der Frau bis zu dem Mann, der viel größer war als ich und mich genau ansah. Dann sprach wieder die Frau.

"Wir wollten Ihnen nur sagen, daß uns das leidtut. Wir hatten uns das nicht so vorgestellt. Nicht alle, die das tragen", sie zeigten auf ihr Parteiabzeichen, "sind mit allem einverstanden, was jetzt geschieht".

Der Mann nickte zustimmend. Ich sah von ihr zu ihm und dann wieder von ihm zu ihr. Auch ich nickte. Ich fühlte, daß ich eigentlich etwas Gewichtiges sagen mußte, aber ich brachte nur ein halblautes "Danke" hervor. Der Mann gab mir die Hand, die Frau berührte mich an der Schulter und sagte: "Viel Glück! Sie werden's brauchen". Dann war es vorbei. Sie gingen weiter und ich ging zurück in die Schlange, wo man mir meinen Platz freigehalten hatte.

Später hat mir jemand gesagt, mit so einer Geste haben der Mann und die Frau weder etwas riskiert, noch habe jemand einen wirklichen Nutzen davon gehabt. Aber das stimmt nicht. Das Risiko mag klein gewesen sein, aber ich spüre bis heute noch, wenn ich mich daran erinnere, wie mich damals diese wenigen Worte aufgemuntert haben. Nicht nur meine Angst war verflogen, ich fühlte mich wieder als Mensch, als mindestens so gut wie meine Nachbarn in der Schlange mit ihren gestanzten silbrigen Hakenkreuzen.[207]

Minna Lachs, who lost her job as a French teacher in a private college, tells of how the school principal and her students, none of whom were Jewish, secretly arranged for the course to continue in her flat and for her to be illegally paid for it. One day on coming home she was warned by the Catholic janitoress not to go upstairs because an SA man was awaiting her arrival on the landing. Despite her acute sense of vulnerability – Minna Lachs was expecting a baby at the time – she climbed the stairs to her flat:

Ich ging die drei Stockwerke hinauf und sah das braune Hemd mit der SA-Binde am Ärmel näherrücken. Und nun stand er auf vor mir in seiner ganzen Größe, der SA-Mann, sagte "Guten Abend" und war ein Mitglied meines Kurses. Um Himmels willen, was hat das zu bedeuten? dachte ich erschrocken, was wird da gespielt? Er klappte sein Buch zu und sagte: "Der Kurs hat mich beauftragt, daß ich, weil ich der einzige Arbeitslose im Kurs bin, Sie überall in Uniform begleiten soll, damit Ihnen in Ihrem Zustand nichts geschieht. Sie wissen ja, was alles auf der Straße passieren kann". Ich weiß nicht mehr, ob es mir gelang, damals die Tränen zurückzuhalten. Er fragte nur: "Wann darf ich morgen kommen, um Sie abzuholen?"

Er begleitete mich tagtäglich auf meinen Gängen zu den Botschaften, zu den Ämtern um das Steuerunbedenklichkeitszeugnis, um den Paß und zu der Speditionsfirma Knauer, die mir ein Bekannter, der im Export arbeitete, empfohlen hatte. [...] Er wartete stets bescheiden draußen, und in den skandinavischen Konsulaten, die ich der Reihe nach "abklapperte", sahen mich die Portiere merkwürdig an, wenn sie bemerkten, daß ich von ihm begleitet wurde. So entstand auch das Gerücht, daß die SA mich geschnappt hätte.[208]

Many Austrians went further than that and took part in acts of resistance and sabotage. A report from the Viennese Gestapo Headquarters to the *Reichssicherheitshauptamt* in Berlin on 11 November, 1941, testifies to this activity:

... Von wesentlich gefährlicher Bedeutung waren indessen die seit Juni 1941 laufend vorgekommenen Sabotageanschläge auf den Waggonpark der Eisenbahn, wo laufend Kupplungsschläuche durchgeschnitten oder Kupplungsringe entfernt, Sand in die Achsenlager der Waggons gestreut oder die Schmierbüchsen der Lokomotiven verstopft wurden, um ein Heiß- oder Auslaufen der Lager herbeizuführen. Der Eisenbahn sind auf dieser Weise in Kärnten erhebliche Mengen an Waggons und Lokomotiven beschädigt worden oder ausgefallen ... Bemerkenswert an dieser Sache ist, daß die Sabotageanschläge immer nur an Waggons verübt werden, die für Wehrmachtszwecke bestimmt sind oder in Richtung Italien laufen ... Das Entfernen oder Vertauschen der Wagenbezettelung schickten diese in andere Richtungen und verursachten einen enormen Aufwand an Nachforschungen.[209]

Many resisted to the point of making the ultimate sacrifice. 2,700 non-Jewish Austrian men and women – Catholics, "Vaterländische", Monarchists, Social Democrats, Communists – were executed for resistance to Nazism, 32,400 died in Gestapo jails and concentration camps and thousands of soldiers were hanged or shot for desertion – so-called "Wehrkraftzersetzung" or "Feigheit vor dem Feinde". The only group about which there are precise statistics consists of members of the Catholic clergy: of the 724 Austrian priests to be imprisoned between 1938 and 1945, 7 died in jail. Fifteen were sentenced to death and executed. Of the 110 that were sent to concentration camps, 90 perished.

The group about which there is least known is that of women, but it might serve as an indication of their suffering that in the "Landesgericht Wien" alone, the same building close to the University of Vienna where Helene Kafka met her death, no fewer than 97 women were decapitated for their part in the resistance.

Theodor Kramer, continuing in the same tradition of liberation poems that was used by Jura Soyfer, Helene Kafka or Käthe Leichter, celebrated the anti-fascist partisans in his poem "Die grünen Kader", written in English exile in the last years of the Second World War. The geographical reference "im Windischen" in the first line locates the action in the border area between Carinthia and Slovenia. The guerilla warfare in Southern Austria against the German army was carried out from 1944 on by Austrians who had deserted from the Wehrmacht and joined the already active resistance movement of the Austro-Slovenians who had been expelled by the Nazis from their Carinthian homeland or seen their relatives transported to extermination camps in order to keep the Greater German Reich "racially pure".[210] As the poem shows, it was not unusual for farmhands and workers to join the partisans spontaneously in their efforts to sabotage electrical and industrial installations:

Wie hoch im Windischen die Berge ragen
und in der Klamm der Wildbach stäubt und rennt,
geschieht es heimlich nun seit vielen Tagen,
daß man die Pfade und die Plätze nennt.
Auf macht vom Zug zur Nacht sich der Verlader,
beim Heuen stiehlt der Jungknecht sich vom Plan,
es hausen tief im Forst die Grünen Kader,
zu ihnen strebt und stößt der Partisan.

Wie sehr im Schlaf die jungen Äste drücken,
wie lang er an den harten Fladen schluckt,
er muß sich nicht mehr vor den Fremden bücken,
wann sie ihn zwingen und ihn Zorn durchzuckt.
Ins Holz zurück ziehn sich die Grünen Kader,
wann sich in losem Schwarm die Truppen nahn;
im Nahkampf läßt sie mit der Axt zur Ader,
vom Fels aus schießt sie ab der Partisan.

Viel ist zu tun noch, klein noch sind die Häufel,
noch rauchen viele Schlote ungesprengt;
den Totenkopf im Wappen führn die Teufel,
geflochten ist der Strick schon, der sie hängt.
Doch einst fügt wieder Quader sich auf Quader
und friedlich knirscht durchs Holz der Säge Zahn;
dann kehrt aus dem Gebirg vom Grünen Kader
müd und zerschunden heim der Partisan.[211]

In another poem in the same collection, "Der Steinbrech", Kramer appeals to the youth of Austria to persevere in their resistance against apparently insurmountable odds, using the metaphor of the saxifrage flower which, though tiny and delicate, manages in time to split the rock. The triple sustenance of the saxifrage – the drop of dew, the buzzard's call, the blue of the sky – evokes by way of simple, pristine images the mountainscapes of Austria in an appeal to the addressees' sense of regional as against pan-German identity:

> Der Steinbrech bricht durchs nackte Felsgestein,
> die Blätter schmal, die Blüten winzig fein;
> so tut die Jugend und ergibt sich nicht
> und zwängt sich durch den kleinsten Spalt zum Licht.
>
> Der Steinbrech wächst und streckt sich allezeit,
> wo keine andre Pflanze sonst gedeiht;
> so tut die Jugend und verzweifelt nie,
> ist es auch kahl und öde rings um sie.
>
> Der Steinbrech braucht nicht viel, ein Tröpfchen Tau,
> den Schrei des Bussards und des Himmels Blau;
> so tut die Jugend und sie fordert nur,
> was Gott verweigert keiner Kreatur.
>
> Den Steinbrech pflückt ein jeder, der da will,
> die Jugend trägt ihn unterm Aufschlag still;
> sie trägt ihn treu, wächst zäh gleich ihm heran,
> bis frei im Land ihn jeder tragen kann.[212]

In other areas, such as the almost impenetrable Alpine slopes and ravines of Salzkammergut, it was Austrian communists who were instrumental in organizing guerilla resistance, with the active or tacit help of numerous individuals of every political shade and social status, including gamekeepers, forest wardens, railwaymen, miners, women from the farming community, parish priests and even disenchanted Nazis and gendarmes. The so-called intelligentsia – teachers and lecturers – were, generally speaking, conspicuously absent, remaining loyal upholders of the Nazi ideology to the end.[213]

6.2 Collaboration

On the whole, the deplorable fact remains that the widespread anti-Semitism prevalent in Vienna up to 1938 greatly facilitated the Anschluss. Worse still, the active

Austrian involvement in bringing about the Holocaust was disproportionately large. As Simon Wiesenthal points out:

> The fact that the plague (of Nazism) originated in Austria is played down. Hitler, Kaltenbrunner, Eichmann, and many others were Austrian. Don't forget that 80% of Eichmann's staff were Austrian, and three quarters of the commanders of extermination camps were also Austrian. Globotchnig, for example, was the chief of Jewish extermination in the General-Gouvernement (Poland), and with a staff of sixty-five people from Carinthia (the region in southern Austria around Klagenfurt) they were responsible for over two million dead. [...] Remember that the Austrian population composed only 8.5% of the population of the Greater German Reich, yet the proportion of Austrians among those who committed crimes was many times greater than that percentage.[214]

Theodor Kramer's wish that all of the commanders and henchmen of the death camps should be brought to justice to answer for the ignominy of Shoah, as passionately expressed in the starkly realistic poem "Der Ofen von Lublin", was not to be satisfied. The five-pointed star in the last stanza is a reference to the liberation of the Majdanek concentration camp by the Red Army in July 1944:

Es steht ein Ofen, ein seltsamer Schacht,
ins Sandfeld gebaut, bei Lublin;
es führten die Züge bei Tag und bei Nacht
das Röstgut in Viehwagen hin.
Es wurden viel Menschen aus jeglichem Land
vergast und auch noch lebendig verbrannt
im feurigen Schacht von Lublin.

Die flattern ließen drei Jahre am Mast
ihr Hakenkreuz über Lublin,
sie trieb beim Verscharren nicht ängstliche Hast,
hier galt es noch Nutzen zu ziehn.
Es wurde die Asche der Knochen sortiert,
in jutene Säcke gefüllt und plombiert
als Dünger geführt aus Lublin.

Nun flattert der fünffach gezackte Stern
im Sommerwind über Lublin.
Der Schacht ist erkaltet; doch nahe und fern
legt Schwalch auf die Länder sich hin,
und fortfrißt, solang nicht vom Henkerbeil fällt
des letzten Schinderknechts Haupt, an der Welt
die feurige Schmach von Lublin.[215]

7. Post-war restoration

In the Nazi registration procedures after the war, 524,000 Austrians were declared to be former Nazis. In 1947, 482,000 of these were pronounced "Minderbelastete" (less incriminated) by a decree of the National Council and had the active and passive right to vote restored to them. They immediately formed a party of the extreme right, *Verband der Unabhängigen*, whose manifesto yet again used catchwords drawn from what Victor Klemperer called "LTI" (Lingua Tertii Imperii, Language of the Third Reich) like "Sauberkeit", "deutsches Volkstum" and "Schicksalsgemeinschaft", as if nothing had happened in the previous years to make such rhetoric forever unusable. In the 1949 elections the *Wahlpartei der Unabhängigen* (forerunner of the *Österreichische Freiheitspartei*) won over 11% of the vote. Between 1945 and 1955, 13,600 Austrians were found by the courts to be guilty of Nazi crimes. Of these, 43 were sentenced to death and 34 to life imprisonment. Those who had been illegal Nazis in the years before the Anschluss – about 100,000 – were initially deprived of their electoral rights and enlisted to perform "deeds of atonement". These already outrageously lenient sentences were in the course of time to be neutralized entirely by generous reprieves.[216] In 1957 all Nazis who had been sentenced to less than eight years hard labour were granted an amnesty and received back-pay for all their years in the public service. In the Sixties and Seventies, most trials against war criminals ended with a verdict of "not guilty". In contrast, many victims of National Socialism had to wait until 1961 for a compensation law (*Abgeltungsfondsgesetz*) to be passed.[217] Groups such as homosexuals, Jehova Witnesses, people who had been sterilized due to the dictates of "racial hygiene" and the relatives of those who were put to death under the Nazi euthanasia programme did not gain "victim" status until 1995. In the case of the gypsies, more than half of Austria's Roma and Sinti population perished in the concentration camps. Yet the campaign for compensation dragged on until 1988, being constantly obstructed by the technicality that Lackenbach, where very many gypsies had been interred in cowsheds and were decimated by outbreaks of typhus, was a "labour" camp as against a "concentration" camp.[218] Of their post-war treatment at the hands of the new "democratic" government, Karin Berger writes:

> 1948 hieß es in einem Schreiben des Innenministeriums an alle Bundespolizeibehörden, daß "das Zigeunerunwesen in einigen Gegenden des Bundesgebietes wieder im Zunehmen begriffen" sei und "sich bereits unangenehm bemerkbar" mache. "Um auf die Bevölkerung Eindruck zu machen", würden sich "Zigeuner oftmals als KZ-ler ausgeben". Für "lästige Zigeuner" faßte man deren "Außerlandsschaffung" ins Auge. Bei Opferrenten und Wiedergutmachungen hatten Roma und Sinti größere Schwierigkeiten als andere ehemalige KZ-Gefangene. Ihre Aussagen wurden angezweifelt, mit viel Aufwand mußten sie nachweisen, vor 1938 in Österreich gelebt zu haben.[219]

The Viennese Romany Ceija Stojka experienced various evictions in the course of her life, some during the Hitler Period, some in the Second Republic. She tells of how her family had to vacate their flat in 1941 and move into a wooden hut in a backyard in the Paletzgasse when she was eight years old, and what happened subsequently:

> Eines Tages holte die Gestapo unseren Vater Karl Wackar Horvath von unserem Platz ab. Sie kamen in einem kleinen Auto und stießen ihn hinein. Wir Kinder standen da, mit Tränen um unseren Vater. Er winkte noch einmal, dann fuhren sie mit ihm fort. Das war 1941 und meine letzte Erinnerung an ihn. Wir sahen ihn nie wieder. Nun wurde uns Kindern die Schule verboten. Die Gestapo legte ein spanisches Gitter um unser kleines Holzhaus und verbot uns, uns außerhalb dieses Gitters aufzuhalten. Ja, wir spürten Auschwitz schon in der Freiheit.[220]

Her father was killed in Dachau, his ashes and a few bone fragments returned to the family in an urn, and she and her family spent the rest of the Hitler Period in Auschwitz, Ravensbrück and Bergen-Belsen. After their liberation and repatriation the family was eventually rehoused in a beautiful flat that had undoubtedly once been in Jewish ownership and expropriated by some National Socialist in the course of the pogroms. What she has to say shows how Austrian "denazification" was often a euphemism for Nazi rehabilitation:

> Am Anfang waren wir 14 Tage dort, acht Tage da, bis endlich die Mama diese freie Nazi-Wohnung gekriegt hat, eine traumhafte Wohnung, dreieinhalb Zimmer, wunderbar. Ein Klavier stand drinnen, das war himmlisch für uns. Circa vier Monate waren wir dort. Dann ist entnazifiziert worden und die Nazis sind wieder zurückgekommen. Wir mußten aus der

Wohnung. Danach wohnten wir noch einige Monate in einer anderen Nazi-Wohnung, dort ist dasselbe passiert. Dann war es aus. Ihr müßt gehen, hat es geheißen, die Wohnung gehört den Leuten, es tut uns leid. Sind wir auf der Straße gestanden.[221]

Ceija Stojka was to go through a second such eviction experience in 1968. In all she received the derisory sum of 30,000 Schilling (the equivalent of $1700 today) as compensation for the loss of her father and her own ordeal as Holocaust victim.

Edward Arie, who was first tortured by SA men in a camp in the Prater and then in Dachau, applied from British exile to the Austrian Government a few years after the war for compensation for what he had suffered at the hands of the SS. In reply he received an application form and a letter asking him to submit evidence that he had been maltreated in Dachau. He tore up the letter. His father, who, as an officer of the Austrian army in the First World War had been decorated for bravery and therefore felt confident enough to stay on in Vienna after the Anschluss, was starved to death in Theresienstadt in 1944.

> In June 1991 it came to his [Edward Arie's] notice that Austria had amended its 1946 law on paying indemnity to victims of Nazism. [...] Fifty-three years later [after his ordeal in Dachau] it seemed as if Austria was willing to compensate him. After seven months of working on his application, the authorities came to the following decision: No compensation is payable for the death of Mr. Arie's father, as Mr. Arie was already over 18 at the time of the father's death; and the adequate compensation for the seven weeks at Dachau should be 1,720 schillings, roughly $150. Edward Arie returned the insulting check with a polite note.[222]

In the post-war period some of the anti-fascist partisans who had risked their lives in combatting the Third Reich suffered *more* discrimination – as communists, or Slovenes, or both – than did the former Nazis, many of whose more powerful exponents soon manœuvred themselves back into prominent positions in trade, industry and the civil service, whereas most resistance fighters fell into oblivion or disrepute, only those who had belonged to the established parties being in any way celebrated. What Peter Kammerstätter, the historian of the Salzkammergut resistance, wrote in 1978 still holds for today:

> So muß festgestellt werden, daß ein großer Teil jener Kräfte, die ihr Leben, ihre Gesundheit für die Beseitigung eingesetzt

haben, unbeachtet und nach dreißig Jahren Ende der NS-Herrschaft oftmals als Verräter bezeichnet werden und fast von allen seit 1945 bestehenden österreichischen Regierungen nicht sehr große Beachtung fanden.[223]

One of the examples of such official disapprobation given by Kammerstätter was that of Frau Elsa Moser, who had been arrested for helping the resistance movement and whose husband Hans, a salt-works official, had been a leading partisan and died in Linz Prison in the Hitler Period. After the establishment of the Second Republic, Frau Moser was notified that her husband had been posthumously relegated to the working-class and that she therefore would only receive the pension of a labourer's widow.[224]

How was this scandalous imbalance possible? First of all, Austrian "denazification", unlike that in Germany, was administered by the post-war authorized Austrian political parties in co-operation with the Allied Forces. The involvement of the indigenous parties led to whitewashing, string-pulling and favouritism, and eventually to a reduction of the whole denazification process to a mere bureaucratic formality. Secondly, the parties felt they had to compete against each other for the considerable electoral potential of those who were still infested with Austro-fascist or Nazi views, and therefore shaped their rhetoric accordingly. After all, according to opinion polls conducted at the end of the Forties, 35% of the Austrian population still felt that National Socialism was basically a good idea that had been carried out wrongly. Anti-Semitism began to re-surface after an indecently short period of respite, even in the form of political posters and propagandist caricatures:

> Bei der Nationalratswahl 1949 wandte sich die ÖVP mit mehreren Plakaten an die ehemaligen Nazis. Eines dieser Plakate zeigte "eine 'huldvolle' ÖVP in Gestalt eines lächelnden Jünglings. Dieser sympathische junge Mann reicht einem armen 'Belasteten' freundlich helfend die Hand. Zwei freche rote Rowdys – als Spezialität mit deutlich gekrümmter Nase als abschreckendem Rassenmerkmal – werfen roten Schmutz auf einen geplagten armen Nazi, obwohl ihm bereits ein Mühlstein um den Hals hängt. Darunter die Lehre: 'Davor schützt dich nur die Österreichische Volkspartei'."[225]

A further reason for the widespread unwillingness on the part of Austrians up to the present day to analyse the past has, according to Gerhard Botz, a very pragmatic basis:

Most of the "Aryanizers" or their descendants are still in possession of the "Jews' houses", "Aryanized" flats, shops, pianos, jewellery and works of art. For years they have viewed with apprehension the possible return of the previous owners, whose property they took at a price certainly far below its true value. This is why there is a reluctance in Austria – especially in Vienna, but also in Salzburg, Graz and other places – to talk about National Socialism, and why the economic aspect of the persecution of the Jews and the specifically Austrian contribution to it are the real "great taboo". This is why the Jews are still feared here.[226]

This probably explains why, as Adi Wimmer has pointed out "to my own and my country's shame", the Jews were never invited back after 1945:

Until recently, as far as Austria's public awareness was concerned, they had no history. For decades after the war there was no public discussion of the meaning and significance of this particular chapter in our history. As we denied to outsiders and repressed within ourselves any Austrian involvement in the horrors of Nazism, we were left no option but to repress the existence of roughly 130,000 of our fellow Austrians in exile. Accepting the mere fact of their existence (let alone welcoming them back home) would have meant assigning them a role in a public discourse which we did our best *not* to have.[227]

Moreover, the American, British and Russian Allies had created a formulation back in 1943 which, in the minds of many Austrians, was to exculpate their country for ever from Nazi involvement. On 1 November at a conference in Moscow, the foreign ministers Hull, Eden and Molotov made a declaration which would have been badly needed in early March 1938 to head off the Anschluss, but in 1943 was hopelessly belated and, in view of the hugely successful nazification of Austria in the first few years following the annexation, a distorted and propagandistic description of the situation, cleverly designed to appeal to the pride of the Austrians hurt by "Prussian" domination. The declaration began with the following sentences:

Die Regierungen Großbritanniens, der Sowjetunion und der Vereinigten Staaten von Amerika kamen darin überein, daß Österreich, das erste Land, das der Hitlerschen Aggression zum Opfer gefallen ist, von der deutschen Herrschaft befreit werden muß.

Sie betrachten den Anschluß, der Österreich am 15. März 1938 von Deutschland aufgezwungen worden ist, als null und nichtig.[228]

It was this formulation which in retrospect was to persuade Austrians at large that they had been *victims* rather than that they had *perpetrated and facilitated the victimization of others* in their own society, and was to be used by Austrian politicians and opinion-makers, from 1945 for decades to come, to redefine the euphoric reception of Hitlerism in March 1938 as an unwanted military occupation and a national humiliation. This proved useful for various governments of the Second Republic in warding off claims for compensation by victims of National Socialism, since the Austrian people *as a whole* had been officially declared to be victims. Peter Utgaard has summarized the interlocking rationalizations of the Austria-as-victim myth:

> Once officially declared a victim, Austria became a liberated rather than a conquered country, Austrian statesmen could argue against reparations or losing territory to Germany's foes during the war, while in domestic politics, Austrian politicians avoided alienating those who were in, or sympathetic to, the Nazi camp. Church leaders, too, contributed to the myth by openly declaring the church and Austrian citizens to be victims of a catastrophe.[229]

Erich Fried, speaking of the immediate post-war years, wrote:

> In Österreich wieder machten es sich allzuviele bequem mit der Behauptung, die bösen Deutschen sei man ja jetzt los und könne sich auf die eigenen gesunden alten Werte besinnen, wobei man vergaß, daß diese gesunden alten Werte auch beim Entstehen des Austrofaschismus, des österreichischen Antisemitismus und auch bei der Erziehung eines Adolf Hitler, Eichmann, Kaltenbrunner oder Seyss-Inquart Pate gestanden hatten [...].[230]

And as Hermann Langbein has written:

> Die österreichische Lebenslüge, die da lautet: "Wir sind 1938 besetzt worden, wir sind 1945 befreit worden, was dazwischen geschehen ist, dafür können wir nichts" hat ihre Kraft erschreckend deutlich bewiesen. Sie wurde die ganzen Jahre hindurch mit Fleiß von Politikern aufgebaut. Und nur zu gern sprach man sie nach. Selbst sich seriös gebende Autoren sprechen von der "Stunde Null" im Jahr 1945, als ob es vorher nichts gegeben hätte, was uns Österreicher betrifft. Damit wird jedes Nachdenken, jede Auseinandersetzung erspart.[231]

Gerhard Amanshauser sarcastically called the rehabilitation of ex-Nazis another form of coming to grips with the past:

Die Leute, die sich geirrt hatten, mußten nicht nur nicht widerrufen, sondern ihr Irrtum erschien bald als respektable Leistung. Man behandelte sie als verdienstvolle Veteranen.
Nachdem die Besatzungsmacht abgezogen war, kamen sie aus ihren Löchern hervor, schüttelten sich die Steifheit aus ihren Gliedern, wurden weltläufig und salonfähig, trugen ihre Trachten zu den Empfängen, rückten in Ehrenstellen und politische Posten nach.

Auch das war eine Form von Vergangenheitsbewältigung.[232]

According to Robert Menasse, the Allies ("Liberators") also continued to play a part in bolstering the myth of Austrian victimhood:

Wir wollten den Nationalsozialismus nicht, wir wurden überfallen und dazu gezwungen! – wurde den Befreiern zugerufen, während man den Österreichern sagte: Wir verstehen schon, daß ihr der "raffinierten massen-psychologischen Goebbelspropaganda" unterlegen seid, die Euch das Paradies auf Erden versprach, niemand wird Euch deshalb einen Strick drehen! Keine Gnade für die Nazis! – wurde proklamiert und gleichzeitig beruhigt: Keine Bange, wir wissen, Ihr habt um das wahre Wesen des National-sozialismus nicht Bescheid gewußt, ihr seid bloß dem "Rattenfänger aus München [!]" auf den Leim gegangen![233]

In the international agreement of 1955 in which the Second Republic was legitimised, Austria was officially exonerated from having to pay reparations to the victims of Nazism. By showing clemency to the Austrians, the Western Allies wanted to secure the loyalty of the new Austrian state to the western political system rather than to that of the other occupier, the Soviet Union.

Fritz Molden, a former member of the resistance movement, said in 1996:

When we returned from the concentration camps in 1945, we thought that, cleared of all co-responsibility by the Allies, we could serve our country best by re-creating a beautiful Austria, a buffer between nations in Central Europe, an island of the blessed in a sea of controversy. Now at last – forty-two years later – the trauma has reached us. We have to face it that our country is not, as President Reagan tried – so kindly – to paint us, made of music, *Sachertorte*, *Lippizaner* and *Sängerknaben* (the famous boys' choir). We have to realize that we are not loved any more and perhaps will not be loved until we face ourselves. For four decades we have overrated ourselves, as did the world. The result is that when we look into the mirror now, we face an ugly image.

Only time and a new image will change this back into an honest face.[234]

But let us return once more to literature to bring home these very points. The Tyrolean playwright Felix Mitterer, born in 1948, took up the theme in his drama *Kein schöner Land*, staged for the first time in the Tiroler Landestheater in 1987. It is based on the true story of an engineer of the name of Rudolf Gomperz, a much honoured public figure in Tyrol because of the huge administrative and consultative contributions he had made towards the development of winter sports and tourism in the area of St. Anton. He was just about to have the title of *Regierungsrat* bestowed upon him when the Anschluss occurred. Though Christian, he was a Jew according to the definitions of the Nuremberg Racial Laws and as such was immediately sacked from his position as director of the St. Anton Tourist Office. He and his non-Jewish wife Maria concocted the story that their two sons were the products of an extramarital affair of hers with an "Aryan", so that the two youths might escape persecution. He had to write over his property into his wife's name to prevent it from being confiscated. A Nazi neighbour, Frau Grete Feldmeier, did not rest until Gomperz was hunted out of St. Anton. In December, 1941, the Gestapo raided his house. Soon afterwards he was ordered to wear the Star of David and to leave by 10 January, 1942, and move to Vienna. He occupied a small flat in the Große Mohrengasse. His wife was told by the Gestapo that she should divorce her husband or else risk being treated as Jewish herself. The matter was solved otherwise: in May, 1942, Rudolf Gomperz was forced to vacate his flat and move to a so-called "Sammellager" in a Viennese schoolhouse, the Sperlschule, to await deportation to Poland. He was seen in Autumn 1942 in the Jewish ghetto of Lemberg (Lwów), Poland, by a woman from St. Anton who was working for the press agency of the Wehrmacht. The incident was related to Hans Thöni:

> Als sie in Begleitung auf der Straße von Lemberg unterwegs war, fiel ihr ein Straßenkehrer auf, den sie sofort als Ing. Gomperz zu erkennen glaubte. Sie ließ ihre Begleiter unter einem Vorwand vorausgehen und sprach den Straßenkehrer an, ob er nicht Ing. Gomperz sei. Er nickte und sprach nur das Wort: "Hunger". Er sah sehr schlecht aus, war unrasiert und stark gebeugt. In der nächsten Bäckerei gab es zwar kein Brot, aber so etwas wie süßes Gebäck. Sie kaufte einen Sack davon und steckte es Gomperz in einer Hauseinfahrt zu. Die Frau wollte gegenüber ihren Begleitern nicht zu erkennen geben, daß sie den Straßenkehrer mit dem Judenstern kannte.[234]

Gomperz is thought to have met his death by being shot in the concentration camp of Minsk.

In Felix Mitterer's play, the Gomperz figure is a cattle-dealer called Stefan Adler. The play opens in an unnamed Tyrolean village in 1933, when Austria was still under the authoritarian Catholic regime of the *Christlichsoziale Partei*, and continues through the Nazi Period. The figure of Rudolf Holzknecht, innkeeper and burgomaster, represents political opportunism. He lives according to the principle spoken to his National Socialist son Erich: "Schlau muaß ma sein, Bua, wenn man in schweren Zeiten überleben will!".[235] In the beginning he has a large portrait of Dollfuß in his pub, and describes himself as "kohlschwarz" while admitting Nazi leanings. After the Anschluss he shows himself to be a consummate "Wendehals", replacing the Dollfuß portrait by one of Hitler and overseeing the marginalization and deportation of his neighbour and former friend Stefan Adler. In the final scene he is wearing an armband with the colours of the Second Republic. He has once more made a smooth transition, this time from Nazism to post-war democracy. His final appearance is immediately preceded by three separate and equally gruelling scenes in which not only Stefan Adler meets a violent end, but also the parish priest is tortured to death and a mentally retarded youth from the village is given a lethal injection as part of the Nazi euthanasia programme. These three scenes are followed by a black-out and a closing of the curtains, to give the audience the impression that the play is over. By this device, the author takes the audience by surprise. The stage directions for the unexpected last scene are as follows:

> *Licht auf den Vorhang, das Publikum beginnt zu applaudieren, weil es glaubt, daß das Stück zu Ende ist. Nach einer Weile kommt zwischen dem Vorhang der Bürgermeister heraus. Er trägt einen Trachtenanzug mit rot-weiß-roter Binde am Arm. Der Bürgermeister winkt lächelnd den Applaus ab.*

Then he gives his speech which treats the theatre audience as if they were the villagers themselves in the immediate post-war period. By this means the author implicates the audience in the general amnesia that befell so many Austrians in the wake of the Second World War. When the play was premièred in the Tiroler Landestheater in 1987, there will certainly have been several people in the audience who had made a similarly artful political transition in 1945 as the Bürgermeister does and resorted to similarly mendacious thought processes and euphemistic rhetoric to justify it:

Danke, danke, danke! (*Applaus verebbt.*) Mitbürger, Freunde, Österreicher! Dank des Vertrauens, das unsere amerikanischen Freunde mir entgegenbringen, bin ich nun wieder euer Bürgermeister! Dieses Vertrauen besteht nicht ohne Grund, wie ich meine! Ihr wißt es selbst, daß ich vielen geholfen habe, in dieser schweren Zeit! Vielen! Ohne Unterschied von Stand und Anschauung, stets um Einigung und Ausgleich bemüht! – Freunde, wir haben alle Furchtbares hinter uns! Viele unserer Söhne – auch mein Sohn! – , viele unserer Väter sind gefallen für eine Idee, an die sie geglaubt haben, mit jeder Faser ihres Herzens! Darum laßt uns ehren diejenigen, die ihre soldatische Pflicht erfüllt haben – in den Tundren des Nordens, in den Schneefeldern Rußlands, im heißen Wüstensand Afrikas! Mag da auch manches passiert sein, was jetzt von manchen breitgetreten und maßlos übertrieben wird – der Krieg, liebe Mitbürger, ist nun einmal kein Honigschlecken! Keinen soll ein Vorwurf treffen! Keinen unserer tapferen Landser, keinen von denen, die in der Heimat in Not und Hunger die Wirtschaftsschlacht schlugen oder in der Verwaltung Ordnung und Gesetz zu vertreten hatten! Denn keiner, keiner von uns wußte, daß wir von einem Wahnsinnigen angeführt wurden! Alle, alle wurden wir mißbraucht; ausgenützt hat man unsere edelsten Gefühle, ausgenützt hat man unseren Idealismus, unseren Glauben, unsere Treue! – Liebe Mitbürger, ich weiß, es gab in dieser schweren Zeit Haß und Streit und Mißgunst in unserem Dorf! Vergessen wir das jetzt, ich appelliere an euch! Streichen wir durch diese Zeit, löschen wir sie aus in unserem Herzen und in unserem Gedächtnis! Vergessen wir Hader und Zwist und kleinliche Rache! Denn nun, Freunde, geht es an den Wiederaufbau; und nur mit vereinten Kräften werden wir diesen Wiederaufbau schaffen! – Darum bitte ich euch: Halten wir alle zusammen, laßt uns gemeinsam, mit neuem Mut, mit neuer Kraft, mit neuem Schaffensdrang das neue, zukünftige Österreich aufbauen! – Ich danke euch![236]

What Felix Mitterer conveys by scenic presentation, Thomas Bernhard spells out in blunt invective:

Die Meinigen sind immer Opportunisten gewesen, ihr Charakter darf ruhig als niedrig bezeichnet werden. Sie paßten sich immer den jeweiligen politischen Verhältnissen an und es war ihnen jedes Mittel recht, einen Vorteil aus gleich was für einem Regime herauszuschlagen. Sie hatten immer zu den gerade an der Macht Befindlichen gehalten und als geborene Österreicher die Kunst des Opportunismus wie keine zweite beherrscht, sie waren politisch nie zu Fall gekommen.[237]

The poet Josef Mayer-Limberg employs a style in imitation of the sociolect of the Viennese working-class district of Ottakring to ridicule what he perceives as an Austrian bent towards apostasy and opportunism:

ösdareicha

noch 18

soziobussla
pfoarafressa

noch 34

sozifressa
pfoaraobussla

noch 38

naziobussla
judnfressa

noch 45

judnobussla
nazifressa

noch 55

ewech neutral
ewech
a schdingada kas[238]

To mark the fiftieth anniversary of the "Reichskristallnacht", the poet Richard Wall of Linz wrote this compilation of actual remarks overheard from older contemporaries speaking in the dialect of the Lower Mühlviertel. They make standard excuses for their passivity in the Hitler Period as their means of "dealing with the past" and even see concentration camps in a favourable light as an effective way of combatting criminality. "Das Gedicht", in the poet's own words, "ist eigentlich eine Montage aus Sätzen, die ich aus den Mündern einiger 'Zeitzeugen', ambivalenter bzw. ambivalent gebliebener 'Nostalgiker' in meiner Jugend und herauf bis zur Gegenwart zu hören bekam (bzw. bekomme)":[239]

Vergangenheitsbewältigung

Mia haum jo nix gwißt
nix genaus haumma ned gwißt
wäu waunsd wos gsogt hesd
do hedns di a glei ghot

an wiez üwa eana
waun den oana von denen gheat hed
des wa scho gnua gwehn
ma hod jo nix sogn deafn gegn eana
des woa ned so wia heid
owa sovü vabrecha hods domoes ned gebn
mid soiche leid wa ma domoes glei ogfoahn
san ma uns ehrli
's gibt vü zvü gsindl heid
's woan jo a vü griminäli im kazet domoes
ned nua lauta politische oda judn
heid wiad des ois aweng üwadriem
ma siachd des ois zu einseitig
san ma uns ehrli
de vün vabrechn des eds mid den vün sex
's geht jo heid ois drunta und drüwa
ois wos recht und sche is
owa untan Hitler heds des ned gebm[240]

Probably one of the most devastating portrayals of the volatile Viennese petit-bourgeoisie capable of effortlessly negotiating the radical political fluctuations of the thirties, forties and fifties is Helmut Qualtinger's and Carl Merz's famous sketch *Der Herr Karl*. George Clare wrote of it:

> Qualtinger's Herr Karl is a portrait true to life, but also one into which the features of the whole Viennese mob of 1938 have been condensed. Mirrored in it are all the nastiness paired with false bonhomie, all the sham *Gemütlichkeit* with its envious vulgarity, of the thousands of Herr Karls and their wives who were now let loose to pour bucketfuls of their hatred over defenceless victims.[241]

The obese Herr Karl, shirking work as an employee in a delicatessen at the beginning of the sixties, chats to the audience about his life in his whining Viennese drawl as if to an invisible young customer. As he tells of how he coasted from the Socialists to the Fatherland Front and then to the Nazis, he ascribes his opportunism and venality euphemistically to the "unpolitical" nature of the Austrians in general:

> De Dreißgerjahr? Da war i sehr oft arbeitslos. Hackenstad. War immer dazwischen arbeitslos. Ein Leben, junger Mensch! Dazwischen arbeitslos, dazwischen hab i was g'habt, arbeitslos ... was g'habt ... oft meine Posten g'wechselt. I war unbeständig ... I war ein Falter.

> Bis Vieradreißig war i Sozialist. Das war aa ka Beruf. Hat ma aa net davon leben können ... heit wenn i war ... aber heit bin i darüber hinaus ... i hab eine gewisse Reife, wo mir de Dinge gegenüber abgeklärt sind ...

Na – im Vieradreißgerjahr ... wissen S' eh, wia des war. Naa,
Sie wissen's net. Se san ja z' jung. Aber se brauchen's aa net
wissen ... Das sind Dinge, da wolln ma net dran rührn, da
erinnert man sich nicht gern daran ... niemand in Österreich
... Später bin i demonstrieren gangen ... für die Heimwehr ...
net? Hab i fünf Schilling kriagt ... Dann bin i ummi zum ... zu
de Nazi ... da hab i aa fünf Schilling kriagt ... naja, Österreich
war immer unpolitisch ... i maan, mir san ja kane politischen
Menschen ... aber a bissel a Geld is z'sammkummen, net?[242]

When recalling the days of the Anschluss, he uses the
colloquial term "Hetz" to refer to the fun had by the Viennese
at the time, inadvertently awakening the associations of that
word with "Hetze" (rabble-rousing) and "Hetzjagd" (hounding).
The eroticizing effect of the Heldenplatz speech is alluded to
obscenely by the suggestion that the young customer was
conceived as an immediate result of it:

Naja – des war eine Begeisterung ... ein Jubel, wie man sie
sich überhaupt nicht vorstellen kann – nach diesen
furchtbaren Jahren ... die traurigen Jahre ... Endlich amal
hat der Wiener a Freid g'habt ... a Hetz ... ma hat was g'segn,
net? Des kennen S'Ihna gar net vurstelln.

Wann san Se geborn? Achtadreißig? Naja, also mir san alle ...
i waaß no ... am Ring und am Heldenplatz g'standen ...
unübersehbar warn mir ... man hat gefühlt, ma is unter sich
... es war wia bein Heirigen ... es war wia a riesiger Heiriger
...! Aber feierlich. Ein Taumel. *Er lacht* Na, drum san se ja
achtadreißig geborn ... Wann? Im Dezember, naja ...[243]

Herr Karl's opinions of Hitler fall back upon the widespread
clichés of the evil seducer and/or the great leader with the
mesmeric gaze:

Na, unsere Polizisten san aa schon da g'standen mit die
Hakenkreuzbinden ... es war furchtbar ... das Verbrechen, wie
man diese gutgläubigen Menschen in die Irre geführt hat ...
Der Führer hat geführt.

Aber a Persönlichkeit war er ... vielleicht ein Dämon ... aber
man hat die Größe gespürt ...

I maan, er war net groß. I bin ja vor ihm g'standen – beim
Blockwartetreffen im Rathaus. So wie i jetzt mit Ihnen sitz,
bin i vor ihm g'standen ... Er hat mi ang'schaut ... mit seinen
blauen Augen ... i hab eahm ang'schaut ... hat er g'sagt:
"Jaja". Da hab i alles g'wußt.[244]

As "Blockwart" it had been Herr Karl's duty to ensure order,
i.e. to see that Jews scrubbed anti-Nazi slogans off the

pavements. While admitting the fun that he had in doing so, he still manages to define himself as "victim" and "idealist":

I maan, schaun S', was ma uns da nachher vorg'worfen hat – des war ja alles ganz anders ... da war a Jud im Gemeindebau, a gewisser Tennenbaum ... sonst a netter Mensch ... da ham s' so Sachen gegen de Nazi g'schrieben g'habt auf de Trottoir ... und der Tennenbaum hat des aufwischen müssen ... net er allan ... de andern Juden eh aa ... hab i ihm hing'führt, daß ers aufwischt ... und der Hausmaster hat zuag'schaut und hat g'lacht ... er war immer bei aner Hetz dabei ...

Nachn Krieg is er z'ruckkumma, der Tennenbaum. Is eahm eh nix passiert ... Hab i ihm auf der Straßen troffen. I gries eahm freundlich: "Habediehre, Herr Tennenbaum!" Der hat mi net ang'schaut. I grüaß ihn no amal: " – 'diehre, Herr Tennenbaum" ... Er schaut mi wieder net an. Hab i ma denkt ... na bitte, jetzt is er bees ... Dabei – irgendwer *hätt's* ja wegwischen müaßn ... i maan, der Hausmaster war ja aa ka Nazi. Er hat's nur net selber wegwischen wolln.

Alles, was man darüber spricht heute, is ja falsch ... es war eine herrliche, schöne ... ich möchte diese Erinnerung nicht missen ... Dabei hab ich ja gar nichts davon g'habt ... Andere, mein Lieber, de ham si g'sund g'stessn ... Existenzen wurden damals aufgebaut ... G'schäften arisiert, Häuser ... Kinos!

I hab nur an Juden g'führt. I war an Opfer. Andere san reich worden. I war Idealist.[...][245]

At the end of the war, Herr Karl quickly learnt the necessary phrases to ingratiate himself with both the Russian and American occupation forces:

Wann a Autobus mit aner russischen Reiseg'sellschaft kumma is, – bin i glei dag'standen, hab g'sagt "Towarischi ... sdrasfudje!" Na ham s' ma auf de Schulter klopft und g'lacht ... da hab i scheen kriegt ... Und de Amis ... wann de kumma san, hab i sogar 's Wagentürl aufg'macht, hab g'sagt "Hello Sör! Everything is O.K. Americans O.K. Look at that Vienna, town of eternal Symphonie and music" ... Des heerns immer gern. Des is scho a Sache, was de auslassn ... ka Vergleich mit de Deitschen. Weil Deitsch kann eh a jeder.[246]

Herr Karl adapts to the Second Republic with equal mutability and is also delighted when the same occupation forces whom he once cheered as liberators are now sent home. He is there at Belvedere Castle on 15 May 1955 when the Austrian Minister for the Exterior, the same Leopold Figl that had suffered torture in Dachau, signs the State Treaty declaring Austria to be a "sovereign, independent and democratic state". Herr Karl hardly differentiates between this celebration and that on 15 March 1938 and distorts Leopold Figl's name:

> G'freit hab i mi scho ... an den Tag, wo ma 'n bekommen ham ... den Staatsvertrag ... Da san ma zum Belvedere zogn ... san dag'standen ... unübersehbar ... lauter Österreicher ... wie im Jahr achtadreißig ... weil's Belvedere is ja klaner als der Heldenplatz. Und die Menschen waren auch reifer geworden ...
>
> Und dann is er herausgetreten ... der ... der ... Poldl und hat die zwa andern Herrschaften bei der Hand genommen und mutig bekannt: "Österreich ist frei!" Und wie i des g'hört hab, da hab i g'wußt: Auch das hab ich jetzt geschafft. Es ist uns gelungen – der Wiederaufbau ...[247]

Helmut Qualtinger has been called "Österreichs schlechtes Gewissen".[248] He is not the only one. The post-war Austrian writers, commentators and historians of the Anschluss quoted in this book are just some of the many voices who have tried to shake the more phlegmatic and forgetful among their fellow countrymen and -women out of their complacency and post-Holocaust rationalizations. One could quote many more. Edith Haider, seven years of age when the Anschluss occurred and therefore plainly innocent, seems never to have overcome the feeling of guilt by association, as her troubled cycle of poems *Besuch in Mauthausen* shows. It was written after she visited the concentration camp at the age of 64. This poem conveys the pain of not being able to undo what was done:

> Wenn Du nicht mehr
> den Krug reichen darfst
> dem Durstigen,
> wenn es Missetat ist,
> das Brot zu brechen dem,
> der da hungert,
> wenn es dir verwehrt ist,
> deinen Mantel zu breiten
> über den, der Kälte leidet,
> nicht ans Herz nehmen darfst
> den Verzweifelten,
> dann hat sich
> die Weltordnung
> verkehrt.
>
> Manche haben es versucht –
> trotz allem –
> doch ihre Zahl reicht nicht aus
> zu rechtfertigen jene,

die gleichgültig
dabeistanden.[249]

But one should perhaps rightly close with an address to the Austrian people written in 1962 by one who was made to bear the full repercussions of the Anschluss. Stella Rotenberg, banned from continuing her medical studies at Vienna University, escaped first to Holland and then to England in March 1939, while many of her nearest relatives chose to remain at home and perished as a result:

Großvater wurde im Jahr 1939, im Krieg gegen Polen, von Wehrmacht- oder Einsatzgruppen erschlagen. Meine Eltern wurden am 20. Mai 1942 von Wien nach Polen verschickt, als Ziel war Izbica bei Sobibor angegeben, sie sollen aber auf dem Weg dorthin aus dem Zug geholt und in einem Wald erschossen worden sein. Vielleicht aber wurde meine Mutter in Auschwitz umgebracht.[250]

This is her poem:

An meine Landsleute

Ich werde alt.
Meine Mutter ist tot.
Meine Mutter lebte vor Jahren.

In einem Mai
bei Morgenrot
kam ein schwarzer Wagen gefahren.

Sieben Männer
mit Koppel und Riem
sprangen ab und waren ihr Geleite

zum Aspangbahnhof
beim Rennweg, in Wien,
und wichen ihr nicht von der Seite.

Verriegelt rechts,
versiegelt links,
im Frachtzug für Pferde und Kohlen,

mit Gefährten verpfercht,
nach Osten gings,
nach Auschwitz im südlichen Polen.

Am vierten Tag
vom Viehwaggon
fielen Lebendige und Leichen.

Der Himmel rußte;
in der Station
stellte ein Mann die Weichen.

Was dann geschah?
Wißt ihr das nicht?
Wollt ihr es wissen? Und sagen?

Ich war nicht dabei.
Es ist alles vorbei.
Ich darf mich nicht beklagen.[251]

The text, in its incisive simplicity, defies commentary. Yes, one can and should point out such contrasting metaphors as the month of May, time of rebirth, and the hearse-like image of "ein schwarzer Wagen" in the second stanza, ironically conflicting with the kitschy imaging of the Anschluss by the Nazis as vernal and even Pentecostal. Perhaps one is also allowed to suggest that not only the largely unfelt guilt of the perpetrators and fellow-travellers is the theme, but that the infinitely more painful sense of guilt felt by the survivors towards the beloved relatives who were not spared is conveyed in the ironic reverberations of the last stanza. Why, the conclusion of the poem prompts us to ask, has the task of "Trauerarbeit" been left to the less unfortunate *victims* rather than to the *perpetrators* of Shoah? One could justifiably invert all three statements made in that last stanza and say that the author was very much "dabei" in her sense of helplessness and remorse, that Nazism in its various manifestations is not by any means "vorbei" in the light of recent developments in the political arena of Austria and elsewhere, and finally that the poet – and particularly this poet – has not only a right but an artistic and human mandate to confront her fellow-Austrians with what many of them have so assiduously repressed. And this she does, in a searing description of those undeniable and, to this very day, insufficiently explained events – events that by no means implicate only the Austria of the past but all of Europe.

Notes

1   Lili Körber, *Eine Österreicherin erlebt den Anschluß*, ed. Viktoria Hertling,
        Vienna/Munich, 1988, p. 48. For the anti-Semitic tendencies of the Austrian
        Ständestaat cf. Jonny Moser, "Die Katastrophe der Juden in Österreich 1938–1945
        – ihre Voraussetzungen und ihre Überwindung", in *Der gelbe Stern in Österreich.
        Katalog und Einführung zu einer Dokumentation. Studia Judaica Austriaca*, vol. V,
        Eisenstadt, 1977, pp. 103–105.

2   *Cf.* Gerhard Botz, *Der 13. März 38 und die Anschlußbewegung. Selbstaufgabe,
        Okkupation und Selbstfindung Österreichs 1918–1945*, Vienna, 1981. See
        particularly Ch. 1: "Der Anschluß als Wunschbild: Anschlußideologie und
        -versuche (1918–1938)", pp. 5–17.

3   Wilhelm J.Wagner, *Der große Bildatlas zur Geschichte Österreichs*, Vienna, 1995, p.
        216.

4   *Cit.* Felix Kreissler, *Von der Revolution zur Annexion. Österreich 1918 bis 1938*,
        Vienna, 1970, p. 287.

5   Joseph Goebbels, *Tagebücher 1924–1945*, ed. Ralf Georg Reuth, Munich/Zurich,
        1992, p. 1208.

6   *Cit.* Christiane Klusacek, Herbert Steiner & Kurt Stimmer (eds.), *Dokumentation zur
        Österreichischen Zeitgeschichte, 1938–1945*, Vienna/Munich, 1980, p. 12.

7   *Cit.* Hans–Harald Müller, "*Mainacht in Wien*. Das Bild des 'Anschlusses' in einem
        Romanfragment von Leo Perutz", in Donald G. Daviau, *Austrian Writers and the
        Anschluß. Understanding the Past – Overcoming the Past*, Riverside, CA, 1991, p.
        187.

8   *Cit.* F.L. Carsten, *Faschismus in Österreich. Von Schönerer zu Hitler*, Munich, 1978,
        p. 293f.

9   Körber, *op.cit.*, p. 68f.

10   *Cit.* Klusacek, Steiner & Stimmer, *op. cit.*, p. 16.

11   Körber, *op. cit.*, p. 92.

12   *Cit.* Erich Scheithauer *et al.*, *Geschichte Österreichs in Stichworten. Teil VI: Vom
        Ständestaat zum Staatsvertrag von 1934 bis 1955*, Vienna, 1984, p. 53f.

13   Goebbels, *op. cit.*, p. 1210.

14   Scheitauer *et al.*, *op. cit.*, p. 59.

15   *Ibid.*

16   Mimi Großberg, *Gedichte und kleine Prosa*, Vienna, 1972, p. 55.

17   Gerda Hoffer, *Nathan ben Simon und seine Kinder. Eine europäisch–jüdische
        Familiengeschichte*, Munich 1996, p. 175f.

18   George Clare, *Last Waltz in Vienna*, London/Basingstoke, 1984, p. 177.

19   Horst–Werner Franke, "'Ich wollte ein Wiener sein.' Die Erinnerungen von Hans

Schauder", in *Das jüdische Echo. Europäisches Forum für Kultur und Politik*, vol, 48 (1999), p. 360.

20   Hilde Spiel, *Die hellen und die finsteren Zeiten. Erinnerungen 1911–1946*, Munich, 1989, p. 174.

21   Gitta Sereny, *The German Trauma: Experiences and Reflections 1938–2000.* Harmondsworth, 2000, p.4f.

21   Willy Stern, "Viele 'Freunde' wurden Feinde", in Willy Kummerer (ed.), *1938–1988. Ein Beitrag der Zentralsparkasse und Kommerzialbank zum Gedenkjahr*, Vienna, 1988, p. 15.

22   Franz Werfel, *Cella oder Die Überwinder. Versuch eines Romans*, Frankfurt a.M., 1982, p. 112.

23   *Ibid.*, p. 113.

24   Körber, *op. cit.*, p. 105f.

25   Robert Breuer, *Nacht über Wien*, Vienna, 1988, p. 31f.

26   G.E.R. Geyde, *Die Bastionen fielen*, Vienna, 1947, p. 281f.

27   Gregor von Rezzori, *Memoiren eines Antisemiten*, excerpted in Ulrich Weinzierl (ed.), *Österreichs Fall. Schriftsteller berichten vom "Anschluß"*, Vienna/Munich, 2nd ed., 1988, p. 78f.

28   Carl Zuckmayer, *Als wär's ein Stück von mir. Horen der Freundschaft*, Frankfurt a.M., 1977, p. 56.

29   Walter Mehring, "Die letzten Stunden", in Weinzierl, *op. cit.*, p. 70.

30   Friedrich Torberg, *Auch das war Wien. Roman*, ed. David Axmann & Edwin Hartl, Munich/Vienna, 1984, pp. 340–341.

31   *Cf.* Karl Marx & Friedrich Engels, *Das kommunistische Manifest*, Leipzig 1976, p. 43, where it is said of the "Lumpenproletariat" that it is, in accordance with its whole situation, more prepared to let itself be bought over to reactionary activities.

32   Zuckmayer, *op. cit.*, p. 56.

33   Zuckmayer, *op. cit.*, p. 61.

34   Scheithauer *et al.*, *op. cit.*, p. 60.

35   *Cit.* Helmut Andics, *Der Staat, den keiner wollte. Österreich von der Gründung der Republik bis zur Moskauer Deklaration*, Munich, 3rd. ed., 1984, p. 277.

36   *Cit.* Ernst Hanisch, *Der lange Schatten des Staates. Österreichische Gesellschaftsgeschichte im zwanzigsten Jahrhundert*, Vienna, 1994, p. 344.

37   *Cit.* Klusacek, Steiner & Stimmer, *op. cit.*, p. 26f.

38   Ernst Lothar, *Das Wunder des Überlebens. Erinnerungen und Ergebnisse*, Vienna/Hamburg, 1961, p. 97.

39   Körber, *op. cit.*, p. 102.

40   *Cit.* Adi Wimmer (ed.), *Strangers at Home and Abroad. Recollections of Austrian Jews Who Escaped Hitler*, tr. Ewald Osers, Jefferson N.C./London, 2000, p. 75.

41   *Cit.* Christiane Klusacek & Kurt Stimmer (ed.), *Dokumentation zur Österreichischen Zeitgeschichte, 1928–1938*, Vienna/Munich, 1982, p. 501.

42   Andics, *op. cit.*, p. 289.

43   Klaus Mann, *Der Vulkan. Roman unter Emigranten*, Berlin/Weimar, 1969, p. 577.

44   *Cit.* Scheithauer *et al.*, *op. cit.*, p. 63.

45   Goebbels, *op. cit.*, p. 1216.

46   Erich Fried, *Mitunter sogar Lachen*, in E.F., *Gesammelte Werke*, ed. Viktor
       Kaukoreit & Klaus Wagenbach, Berlin, 1993, p. 547f.

47   *Ibid.*

48   Cf. Friedrich Jenaczek, "Zeittafel", in Joesf Weinheber, *Gedichte*, ed. Friedrich
       Sacher, 2nd edition, Hamburg, 1978, p. 457.

49   In Heinz Kindermann (ed.), *Heimkehr ins Reich. Großdeutsche Dichtung aus
       Ostmark und Sudentenland 1866–1938*, Leipzig, 1939, p. 326f..

50   *Ibid.*, p. 329f.

51   In Bund deutscher Schriftsteller Österrichs (ed.) *Bekenntnistuch österreichischer
       Dichter*, Vienna, 1938, p. 78.

52   Kindermann, *op. cit.,* p. 332.

53   In Bund deutscher Schriftsteller Österreichs (ed.), *op cit.*, p. 104.

54   Zuckmayer, *op. cit.*, p. 55.

55   Torberg, *op. cit.*, p. 316.

56   *Cit.* Klusacek, Steiner & Stimmer, *op. cit.*, p. 31f.

57   Torberg, *op. cit.*, p. 326f.

58   Minna Lachs, *Warum schaust du zurück? Erinnerungen 1907–1941*,
       Vienna/Munich/Zurich, 1986, p. 184.

59   *Cit.* Klusacek, Steiner & Stimmer, *op. cit.*, p. 32f.

60   In his commentary "mein gedicht und sein autor" written in 1967, Jandl presents
       himself as having been fourteen in the Spring of 1938, in Ernst Jandl: *Gesammelte
       Werke*, ed. Klaus Siblewski, vol. 3: *Stücke und Prosa*, Darmstadt & Neuwied 1985,
       p. 470. According to Kristina Hewig, Jandl was born on 1 August 1925, which
       would mean that he was twelve at the time of Hitler's Heldenplatz speech. (See
       Kristina Hewig, *Ernst Jandl. Versuch einer Monographie*. phil. Diss. Vienna 1981, p.
       24.)

61   Jandl, *op. cit.*, vol. 1: *Gedichte*, p. 124.

62   Ernst Hanisch, "Einleitung des Gesellschaftshistorikers", in: Walter Weiss & Ernst
       Hanisch (ed.), *Vermittlungen. Texte und Kontexte österreichischer Literatur im
       zwangzigsten Jahrhundert*, Salzburg/Vienna, 1990, p. 12.

63   Jandl, *op. cit.*, p. 470.

64   Jörg Drews, "Über ein Gedicht von Ernst Jandl: 'wien: heldenplatz'", in Wendelin
       Schmidt–Dengler (ed.): *Ernst Jandl Materialienbuch*, Darmstadt/Neuwied, 1982, p.
       35.

65   Jürgen Koppensteiner: "'juble und jodle!' Fünf Gedichte für eine Österreich–
       Landeskunde", in *Die Unterrichtspraxis*, vol. 20, Nr. 2 (1987), p. 245.

66   *Cf.* Ernst Jandl, *op. cit.*, pp. 480–490.

67   Ulrich Greiner, "gottelbock. Hitlers Rede in Wien und ein Gedicht von Ernst Jandl",
       in *Die Zeit*, Nr. 11, March 11, 1988.

68   Rudolfine Haiderer: *Grüß Gott! Heil Hitler! Freundschaft! Erlebnisse eines Wiener
       Arbeiterkindes 1926–1945*, Krems, 1995, p. 72.

69   *Cit.* Jochen Steinmayr: "Vier Tage, die Österreich berauschten. Ein halbes
       Jahrhundert später erinnern sich Zeugen an Hitlers Triumphzug nach Wien", in:

	Die Zeit, Nr. 11, March 11, 1988.
70	Elfriede Schmidt, *1938 ... and the Consequences. Questions and Answers,* trans. Peter J. Lyth, Riverside, CA, 1992, p. 248f.
71	Andics, *op. cit.*, p. 288.
72	*Cf.* Oliver Rathgorb, Wolfgang Duchkowitsch, Fritz Hausjell (ed.), *Die veruntreute Wahrheit. Hitlers Propagandisten in Österreich '38*, Salzburg, 1988, p. 72f.
73	*Cf.* Drews, *op. cit.*, p. 36: "Steht es ['zirka'] abschwächend dazu – à la: es war gar nicht der *ganze* Heldenplatz von Menschen erfüllt?"
74	Peter Pabisch: "Sprachliche Struktur und assoziative Thematik in Ernst Jandls experimentellem Gedicht 'wien: heldenplatz', in *Modern Austrian Literature*, vol. 9, Nr. 2 (1976), p. 82.
75	*Ibid.*
76	Jandl, *op. cit.*, p. 471.
77	Pabisch, *op. cit.*, p. 78.
78	*Cf.* Drews, *op. cit.*, p. 36f.
79	Erich Fromm, *Anatomie der menschlichen Destruktivität*, Reinbek, 1977, p. 474.
80	*Ibid.*, p. 479.
81	*Cf.* Pabisch, *op. cit.*, p. 81.
82	Zuckmayer, *op. cit.*, p. 69.
83	In Kindermann (ed.), *op. cit.,* p. 346.
84	*Cit.* Hanisch, *op. cit.*, p. 344.
85	Lachs, *op. cit.*, p. 193.
86	Franz Werfel, *Cella oder Die Überwinder. Versuch eines Romans*, Frankfurt a.M., 1982, p. 114.
87	Torberg, *op. cit.*, p. 338f.
88	Clare, *op. cit.*, p. 195.
89	See Jandl, *op. cit.*, p. 471.
90	*Cf.* Drews, *op. cit.*, p. 38.
91	Pabisch, *op. cit.*, p. 82f.
92	Jandl, *op. cit.*, p. 471.
93	Fromm, *op. cit.* See especially Ch. 13: "Bösartige Aggression: Adolf Hitler, ein klinischer Fall von Nekrophilie", pp. 415–486.
94	Drews, *op. cit.*, p. 39.
95	*Ibid.*
96	Jandl, *op. cit.*, p. 470.
97	Victor Klemperer, *"LTI". Die unbewältigte Sprache. Aus dem Notizbuch eines Philologen*, Munich, 1969, p. 116.
98	*Ibid.*, p. 118.
99	*Cit.* Walter Weiss & Ernst Hanisch, *op. cit.*, p. 197.
100	*Ibid.*, p. 200.
101	*Cit.* Fritz M. Rebhahn, *Die braunen Jahre. Wien 1938–1945*, Vienna, 1995, p. 15.
102	*Cit.* Erich Fried, "Die Postkarte", in E.F., *op. cit.*, p. 638.
103	*Cit.* Helmut Gamsjäger, *Die Evangelische Kirche in Österreich in den Jahren 1933 bis 1938 unter besonderer Berücksichtigung der Auswirkungen der deutschen*

Kirchenwirren, phil. Diss. Vienna 1967, p. 132.

104   In Kindermann (ed.), *op. cit.*, p. 349.

105   Ulrich Weinzierl, "Die Iden des März", in Weinzierl, *op. cit.*, p. 170.

106   Pabisch *op. cit.*, p. 82.

107   Manès Sperber, *Wie eine Träne im Ozean. Romantrilogie. 2. Buch: Tiefer als der Abgrund*, Munich, 1980, p. 492.

108   Torberg, *op. cit.*, p. 340.

109   Sperber, *op. cit.*, p. 493.

110   *Ibid.*

111   Elisabeth Castonier, *Stürmisch bis heiter: Memoiren einer Außenseiterin*, Munich, 1964, p. 260.

112   Körber, *op. cit.*, p. 53.

113   Horst-Werner Franke, *op. cit.*, p. 352.

114   Breuer, *op. cit.*, p. 46.

115   *Cit.* Weinzierl, *op. cit.*, p. 163

116   Gerhard Bronner, "Ihr werdet's halt provoziert haben", in *Profil*, Nr. 34 (1987), p. 16f.

117   Adi Wimmer, "Introduction", in A.W. (ed.), *op. cit.*, p. 8.

118   Erwin Hartl, "Was mag sich Friedrich Torberg gedacht haben", epilogue to Torberg, *op. cit.*, p. 377.

119   Adi Wimmer, *op. cit.*, p. 66f.

120   Manès Sperber, "All das Vergangene"..., in M.S., *Bis man mir die Scherben auf die Augen legt*, Zurich, 1984, p. 764f.

121   *Cit.* Scheitauer et al., *op. cit.*, p. 66.

122   *Cit.* Gerhard Botz, *Wien vom "Anschluß" zum Krieg. Nationalsozialistische Machtübernahme und politisch-soziale Umgestaltung am Beispiel der Stadt Wien 1938/39*, Vienna/Munich, 1978, p. 123.

123   *Cit. ibid.*, p. 126.

124   *Cit.* Herbert Rosenkranz, *Verfolgung und Selbstbehauptung. Die Juden in Österreich 1938-1945*, Vienna/Munich, 1978, p. 25.

125   *Ibid.*

126   See Jeanne Benay (ed.), *L'Autriche 1918-1938*, Rouen, 1998, p. 352.

127   Andics, *op. cit.*, p. 306.

128   Geyde, *op. cit.*, p. 295.

129   Ulrich Becher & Peter Preses, *Der Bockerer. Eine tragische Posse*, Reinbek, 1981, pp. 16-18.

130   Zuckmayer, *op. cit.*, p. 539.

131   Stella Rotenberg, "Deutsche Nacht", in S.R., *Scherben sind endlicher Hort. Ausgewählte Lyrik und Prosa*, ed. Primus-Heinz Kucher & Armin A. Wallas, Vienna, 1991, p. 31.

132   Lachs, *op. cit.*, p.201.

133   *Cit.* Rosenkranz, *op. cit.*, p. 42f.

134   Fred Wander, *Das gute Leben. Erinnerungen*, Munich/Vienna, 1996, p. 21.

135   Alois Vogel, *Schlagschatten - Totale Verdunkelung. Zwei Romane*, ed. August

	Obermayer & Wen delin Schmidt–Dengler, Vienna/Munich, 1999, pp. 446–448.
136	Sereny, *op. cit.*, p. 6.
136	Daniel Goldhagen, *Hitler's Willing Executioners*, New York, 1996.
137	Gerhard Botz, "The Dynamics of Persecution in Austria, 1938–45", in Robert S. Wistrich (ed.), *Austrians and Jews in the Twentieth Century. From Franz Joseph to Waldheim*, New York, 1992, p. 214.
138	*Cit.* Botz, *Wien vom "Anschluß" zum Krieg*, p. 248.
139	*Cit.* Benay, *op. cit.*, p. 353.
140	Joseph Roth, *Werke*. Vol. 3: *Das journalistische Werk 1929–1939*, ed. K. Westermann, Cologne, 1991, p. 795.
141	Richard Schifter, Foreword to Elfriede Schmidt, *op. cit.*, p. 1.
142	Stefan Zweig, *Die Welt von gestern. Erinnerungen eines Europäers*, Vienna, 1948, p. 541.
143	In Kummerer, *op. cit.*, p. 15.
144	*Cit.* Peter Malina & Gustav Spann, *1938 – 1988. Vom Umgang mit unserer Vergangenheit*, Vienna, 1988, p. 5.
145	*Cit.* Gerhard Schönberner (ed.), *Wir haben es gesehen. Augenzeugenberichte über Terror und Judenverfolgung im Dritten Reich*, Hamburg, 1962, p. 78.
146	Ruth Klüger, *weiter leben. Eine Jugend*, Munich, 1997, pp. 46–49.
147	See Paul Huber, Gregor Ryndziak and Michael Adler, *FK AUSTRIA MEMPHIS Klubgeschichte*, at www.telecom.at/fak/geschichte/mitte.html
148	Friedrich Torberg, "Auf den Tod eines Fußballspielers", in Mimi Großberg, *Geschichte im Gedicht. Das politische Gedicht der Austro–Amerikanischen Exilautoren des Schicksalsjahres 1938*, New York, 1982, p. 16f.
149	Wilhelm Szabo, "Nach dem Entscheid", in Arthur West (ed.), *Linkes Wort für Österreich*, Vienna, 1985, p. 53.
150	Max Mell, "Am Tage der Abstimmung. 10. April 1938", in: Kindermann (ed.), *op. cit.*, p. 360.
151	*Ibid.*
152	Franz Kain, *Am Taubenmarkt*, Vienna/Linz/Weitna, 1991, p. 83.
153	Elizabeth Welt Trahan, *Walking with Ghosts. A Jewish Childhood in Wartime Vienna*, New York etc, 1998, p. 63.
154	*Ibid.*, p. 63f.
155	Theodor Kramer, *Wien 1938. Die grünen Kader*, Vienna, 1946, p. 34.
156	Ilse Aichinger, *Die größere Hoffnung. Roman*, Frankfurt a.M., 1991, p. 46f.
157	From "Der gute Ort zu Wien", in Stefan Zweig, *Das lyrische Werk (c)*, Frankfurt a.M., 1967, p. 479.
158	Erich Fried, "Trost", in E.F., *Gesammelte Werke*, vol. III: *Prosa*, p. 616.
159	Erich Fried, *Gesammelte Werke*, vol. I: *Gedichte*, ed. Volker Kaukoreit & Klaus Wagenbach, Berlin, 1993, p. 85.
160	Zweig, *Die Welt von gestern*, p. 540.
161	Kramer, *op. cit.*, p. 55.
162	Friedrich Bergammer, " Erster Spaziergang nach der Verfolgung", in F.B., *Flügelschläge*, Vienna, 1971, p. 10.

163   See letter to Emmy Ferand, 17/8/38, in Hermann Broch, *Gesammelte Werke*, vol. 8: *Briefe von 1929 bis 1951*, ed. Robert Pick, Zurich, 1957, p. 164.

164   Hermann Broch, *Gedichte*, Frankfurt am Main, 1980, p. 43.

165   *Cit.* Manfred Jochum, *Die 1. Republik in Dokumenten und Bildern*, Vienna, 1983, p. 246.

166   Alfred Maleta, "Bewältigte Vergangenheit", in Kummerer, *op. cit.*, p. 21f.

167   *Cit.* Stefan Keller, *Grüningers Fall. Geschichten von Flucht und Hilfe*, Zurich, 3rd ed., 1994, p. 103.

168   *Cit.* Benay, *op. cit.*, p. 354f.

169   *Cit. ibid.*, p. 355.

170   Hoffer, *op. cit.*, p. 175.

171   *Cit.* in *Anschluß 1938*, ed. Dokumentationsstelle des österreichischen Widerstandes, Vienna, 1988, p. 514.

172   *Cit.* Frederick Ungar (ed.), *Austria in Poetry and History*, New York, 1984, pp. 284–6.

173   *Cit.* P. Antonio Sargardoy, *Gelegen und Ungelegen. Die Lebenshingabe von Sr. Restituta*, Vienna, 1996, p.53.

174   *Cit.* Botz, *Der 13. März*, p. 36.

175   Helene Kafka,"Soldatenlied", in Ungar, *op. cit.*, pp. 278–280.

176   Körber, *op. cit.*, p. 120.

177   *Cit.* Sagardoy, *op. cit.*, p. 98f.

178   Wagner, *op. cit.*, p. 224.

179   Berthold Viertel, "Das anständige Leben", in B.V., *Daß ich in dieser Sprache schreibe. Gesammelte Gedichte*, ed. Günther Fetzer, Munich 1981, *cit.* in Klaus Schöffling & Hans J. Schütz (ed.), *Almanach der Vergessenen*, Munich, 1985, p. 35f.

180   Leo Perutz, "Ringsum Stacheldraht. Aus dem Romanfragment 'Mainacht in Wien', geschrieben im Jahr 1938 – II. Teil", in *Die Presse*, April 23/24, 1988.

181   Clare, *op. cit.*, p. 205f.

182   Desider Furst & Lilian R. Furst, *Home is Somewhere Else. Autobiography in Two Voices*, New York, 1994, p. 22.

183   Breuer, *op. cit.*, p. 37.

184   Clare, *op. cit.*, p. 199f.

185   Cit. Dermot Keogh, *Jews in Twentieth–Century Ireland. Refugees, Anti–Semitism and the Holocaust*, Cork, 1998, p. 161.

186   Hubert Butler, "The Kagran Gruppe" (1988), in H.B., *Independent Spirit – Essays*, New York, 1996, p. 364.

187   Clare, *op cit.*, p. 206.

188   Butler, *op. cit.*, p. 365f.

189   Stefan Zweig, *op. cit.*, p. 544.

190   *Ibid.*, p. 545f.

191   *Cit.* Erwin Chvojka, "Versuch, das Wuchern von Legenden zu verhindern. Beiträge zu einer Lebensgeschichte Theodor Kramers", in Konstantin Kaiser (ed.), *Theodor Kramer 1897 –1958. Dichter im Exil. Aufsätze und Dokumente*, in *Zirkular*, special

issue 4, June 1983, p. 69. *Cf.* also Erwin Chvojka & Konstantin Kaiser, *Vielleicht habe ich es leicht, weil schwer, gehabt. Theodor Kramer, 1897–1958. Eine Lebenschronik*, Vienna, 1997, esp. pp. 45ff.

192   *Ibid.*

193   *Ibid.*, p. 71.

194   From Theodor Kramer, "Bitte an die Freunde", in Th.K., *op. cit.*, p. 31.

195   Kramer, *op. cit.*, p. 14.

196   *Ibid.*, p. 21.

197   Erwin Chvojka, *Die Welt will ich behalten. Gedichte aus vierzig Jahren*, Vienna, 1984. Reprinted in *Mit der Ziehharmonika. Zeitschrift für Literatur des Exils und des Widerstands*, vol. 16, Nr. 1 (1999), p. 18.

198   *Cit.* Herbert Steiner (ed.), *Käthe Leichter: Leben und Werk*, Vienna, 1973, p. 179.

199   *Cit. ibid.*, p. 184.

200   *Cit. ibid.*, p. 203f.

201   *Cit. ibid.*, p. 209.

202   See Hugo Gold, *Geschichte der Juden in Wien*, Tel–Aviv, 1966, p. 127.

203   Mimi Großberg, "Israelitisches Blindeninstitut, Hohe Warte, Wien, 1957", in M.G., *Gedichte und kleine Prosa*, p. 59.

204   Rotenberg, *op. cit.*, p. 42f.

205   *Cit.* Kummerer, *op. cit.*, p. 35.

206   *Ibid.*

207   Fried, *op. cit.*, p. 637f.

208   Lachs, *op. cit.*, p. 197.

209   *Cit.* Isabella Ackerl & Walter Kiendel, *Die Chronik Österreichs*, Vienna, 1994, p. 530.

210   For an account of the freedom struggle in Carinthia see the chapter entitled "Das österreichische Bataillon" in Karel Prusnik–Gasper, *Gemsen auf der Lawine. Der Kärtner Partisanenkampf*, Klagenfurt, 1980, pp. 255–265. For a general overview of the various facets of Austrian resistance see Erika Weinzierl, "Der österreichische Widerstand gegen den Nationalsozialismus 1938–1945", in: Erich Zöllner (ed.), *Revolutionäre Bewegungen in Österreich*, Vienna, 1981, pp. 163–175.

211   Theodor Kramer, *op. cit.*, p. 70.

212   *Ibid.*, p. 65.

213   See Hubert Hummer, "Region und Widerstand. Am Beispiel des Salzkammergutes. Der österreichische Widerstand gegen den Nationalsozialismus und seine Verankerung im kollektiven Gedächtnis", in Hubert Hummer, Reinhard Kannonier & Brigitte Kepplinger, *Die Pflicht zum Widerstand*, Vienna, 1986, pp. 139–142.

214   "'... Thanks to Cardinal König a lot has happened ...'. Conversations with Simon Wiesenthal on 24 June and 20 August 1987", in Elfriede Schmidt, *op. cit.*, p. 301.

215   Theodor Kramer, "Der Ofen von Lublin", in Th. K., *op. cit.*, p. 60.

216   *Cf.* Malina & Spann, *op. cit.*, p. 29f.

217   *Cf.* Brigitte Galanda, "Die Maßnahmen der Republik Österreich für die Widerstandskämpfer und Opfer des Nationalsozialismus", in Sebastian Meissl, Klaus–Dieter Mulley & Oliver Rathkolb (ed.), *Verdrängte Schuld, verfehlte Sühne. Entnazifizierung in Österreich 1945–1955*, Vienna, 1986, p. 148.

218   See Forum Politische Bildung (ed.), *Wieder gut machen? Enteignung Zwangsarbeit Entschädigung Restitution*, Innsbruck/Vienna, 1999.

219   Karin Berger: "Vorwort", in Ceija Stojka, *Wir leben im Verborgenen: Erinnerungen einer Rom–Zigeunerin*, ed. Karin Berger, Vienna, 1988, p. 12.

220   Stojka, *op cit.*, p. 16f.

221   *Ibid.*, p. 139f.

222   Adi Wimmer, "Introduction", in A.W., *op. cit.*, p. 5.

223   Peter Kammerstätter, *Materialiensammlung über den Widerstands– und Partisanenbewegung WILLY–FRED, Freiheitsbewegung im oberen Salzkammergut – Ausseerland 1943–1945. Ein Beitrag zur Erforschung dieser Bewegung*, Linz, 1978, p. 17.

224   See *ibid.*, p. 361.

225   Leopold Spira, *Feindbild "Jud". 100 Jahre Antisemitismus in Österreich*, Vienna/Munich, 1981, p. 104. Spira quotes from Dieter Stiefel, *Entnazifierung in Österreich*, Vienna, 1981, p. 317f.

226   Gerhard Botz, "The Dynamics of Persecution in Austria, 1938–45", in Wistrich, *op. cit.*, p. 215.

227   Adi Wimmer, "Introduction", in A.W., *op. cit.*, p.2.

228   *Cit.* Peter Malina & Gustav Spann, *op. cit.*, p. 28.

229   Peter Utgaard, "From *Blümchenkaffee* to *Wiener Melange*: Schools, Identity and Birth of the 'Austria–as–Victim' Myth, 1945–55", in *Austrian History Yearbook*, vol. 30 (1999), p. 131f.

230   Erich Fried, "Klarheit oder Gewöhnung. Gedanken zu Kultur, Politik, Psychologie", in E.F., *Nicht verdrängen, nicht gewöhnen. Texte zum Thema Österreich*, ed. Michael Lewin, Vienna, 1987, p. 110f.

231   Hermann Langbein, "Darf man vergessen?", in Anton Pelinka & Erika Weinzierl (ed.), *Das große Tabu. Österreichs Umgang mit seiner Vergangenheit*, Vienna, 1987, p. 13.

232   Gerhard Amanshauser, "Über Nationalgefühl im allgemeinen und österreichisches Nationalgefühl im besonderen", in Jochen Jung (ed.), *Glückliches Österreich. Literarische Besichtigung unseres Vaterlandes*, Vienna, 1995, p. 21.

233   Robert Menasse, "Im Anfang war das Neue Österreich. Die Erschaffung des österreichischen Überbaus", in: R.M., *Überbau und Underground. Die sozialpartnerische Ästhetik. Essays zum österreichischen Geist*, Stuttgart, 1997, p. 120.

234   *Cit.* Sereny, *op. cit.*, p. 249f.

234   Hans Thöni, "Der Anlaß zum Stück: Das Schicksal des Rudolf Gomperz", in Felix Mitterer, *Kein schöner Land. Ein Theaterstück und sein historischer Hintergrund*, Innsbruck, 1987, p. 117.

235   Mitterer, *op. cit.*, p. 20.

236   *Ibid.*, p. 85f.

237   Thomas Bernhard, *Auslöschung*, *cit.* Regina Kecht, "Faschistische Familienidyllen – Schatten der Vergangenheit in Henisch, Schwaiger und Reichart", in Donald G. Daviau, *op.cit.*, p. 313.

238   Josef Mayer–Limberg, "ösdareicha", in J. M.–L., *Fon da Mõada und de Hausmasda: Gedichda aus Oddagring*, Graz, 1979, reprinted in *Austrian Poetry Today / Österreichische Lyrik heute*, ed. and trans. Milne Holton & Herbert Kuhner, New York, 1985, p. 112f.

239   Letter to Eoin Bourke, 19 January, 1998.

240   Richard Wall, "Vergangenheitsbewältigung", written on 10 November, 1988. From the original manuscript.

241   Clare, *op. cit.*, p. 190.

242   Helmut Qualtinger, *Der Herr Karl*, in *Qualtingers beste Satiren. Vom Travnicek zum Herrn Karl*, ed. Brigitte Erbacher, Frankfurt a.M., 1976, p. 223f.

243   *Ibid.*, p. 226f.

244   *Ibid.*, p. 227.

245   *Ibid.*, p. 228f.

246   *Ibid.*, p. 231.

247   *Ibid.*, p. 233.

248   In "Über dieses Buch", *ibid.*, frontispiece.

249   Edith Haider, "August 1995. Gedichte", in *Mit der Ziehharmonika. Zeitschrift für Literatur des Exils und des Widerstands*, vol. 16, Nr. 3 (1999), p. 24.

250   *Cit.* Armin A. Wallas, "'Dennoch schreibe ich' – eine Annäherung an das literarische Werk von Stella Rotenberg", in Rotenberg, *op. cit.*, p.179.

251   Rotenberg, *op. cit.*, p. 32f.

Works Cited

Ackerl, Isabella & Kiendel, Walter, *Die Chronik Österreichs*, Vienna, 1994.

Aichinger, Ilse, *Die größere Hoffnung. Roman*, Frankfurt a.M., 1991.

Amanshauser, Gerhard, "Über Nationalgefühl im allgemeinen und österreichisches Nationalgefühl im besonderen", in Jochen Jung (ed.), *Glückliches Österreich. Literarische Besichtigung unseres Vaterlandes*, Vienna, 1995.

Andics, Helmut, *Der Staat, den keiner wollte. Österreich von der Gründung der Republik bis zur Moskauer Deklaration*, 3rd ed., Munich, 1984.

Becher, Ulrich & Preses, Peter, *Der Bockerer. Eine tragische Posse*, Reinbek, 1981.

Benay, Jeanne (ed.), *L'Autriche 1918–1938*, Rouen, 1998.

Bergammer, Friedrich, *Flügelschläge*, Vienna, 1971.

Berger, Karin, "Vorwort", in Ceija Stojka, *Wir leben im Verborgenen: Erinnerungen einer Rom-Zigeunerin*, ed. Karin Berger, Vienna, 1988.

Bernhard, Thomas, *Auslöschung*, cit. Regina Kecht, "Faschistische Familienidyllen - Schatten der Vergangenheit in Henisch, Schwaiger und Reichart", in Donald G. Daviau, *Austrian Writers and the Anschluß. Understanding the Past - Overcoming the Past*, Riverside, CA., 1991.

Botz, Gerhard, *Der 13. März 38 und die Anschlußbewegung. Selbstaufgabe, Okkupation und Selbstfindung Österreichs 1918-1945*, Vienna, 1981.

Botz, Gerhard, "The Dynamics of Persecution in Austria, 1938–45", in Robert S. Wistrich (ed.), *Austrians and Jews in the Twentieth Century. From Franz Joseph to Waldheim*, New York, 1992.

Botz, Gerhard, *Wien vom "Anschluß" zum Krieg. Nationalsozialistische Machtübernahme und politisch-soziale Umgestaltung am Beispiel der Stadt Wien 1938/39*, Vienna/Munich, 1978.

Breuer, Robert, *Nacht über Wien*, Vienna, 1988.

Broch, Hermann, *Gedichte*, Frankfurt am Main, 1980.

Broch, Hermann, *Gesammelte Werke*, vol. 8: *Briefe von 1929 bis 1951*, ed. Robert Pick, Zurich, 1957.

Bronner, Gerhard, "Ihr werdet's halt provoziert haben", in *Profil*, Nr. 34, 1987.

Bund deutscher Schriftsteller Österreichs (ed.), *Bekenntnisbuch österreichischer Dichter*, Vienna, 1938.

Butler, Hubert, "The Kagran Gruppe", in H.B., *Independent Spirit - Essays*, New York, 1996.

Carsten, F.L., *Faschismus in Österreich. Von Schönerer zu Hitler*, Munich, 1978.

Castonier, Elisabeth, *Stürmisch bis heiter: Memoiren einer Außenseiterin*, Munich, 1964.

Chvojka, Erwin, *Die Welt will ich behalten. Gedichte aus vierzig Jahren*, Vienna, 1984.

Chvojka, Erwin, "Versuch, das Wuchern von Legenden zu verhindern. Beiträge zu einer Lebensgeschichte Theodor Kramers", in Konstantin Kaiser (ed.), *Theodor Kramer 1897–1958. Dichter im Exil. Aufsätze und Dokumente*, in *Zirkular*, special issue 4, June 1983.

Chvojka, Erwin & Kaiser, Konstantin, *Vielleicht habe ich es leicht, weil schwer, gehabt. Theodor Kramer, 1897-1958. Eine Lebenschronik*, Vienna, 1997.

Clare, George, *Last Waltz in Vienna*, London/Basingstoke, 1984.

Daviau, Donald G., *Austrian Writers and the Anschluß. Understanding the Past - Overcoming the Past*, Riverside, CA., 1991.

Dokumentationsstelle des österreichischen Widerstandes (ed.), *Anschluß 1938*, Vienna, 1988.

Drews, Jörg, "Über ein Gedicht von Ernst Jandl: 'wien: heldenplatz'", in Wendelin Schmidt-Dengler (ed.), *Ernst Jandl Materialienbuch*, Darmstadt/Neuwied, 1982.

Franke, Horst-Werner, "'Ich wollte ein Wiener sein'. Die Erinnerungen von Hans Schauder", in *Das Jüdische Echo. Europäisches Forum für Kultur und Politik*, vol. 48 (1999).

Fried, Erich, *Gesammelte Werke*, ed. Viktor Kaukoreit & Klaus Wagenbach, Berlin, 1993.

Fried, Erich, "Klarheit oder Gewöhnung. Gedanken zu Kultur, Politik, Psychologie", in E.F., *Nicht verdrängen, nicht gewöhnen. Texte zum Thema Österreich*, ed. Michael Lewin, Vienna, 1987.

Fromm, Erich, *Anatomie der menschlichen Destruktivität*, Reinbek, 1977.

Forum Politische Bildung (ed.), *Wieder gut machen? Enteignung Zwangsarbeit Entschädigung Restitution*, Innsbruck/Vienna, 1999.

Furst, Desider & Furst, Lilian R., *Home is Somewhere Else. Autobiography in Two Voices*, New York, 1994.

Galanda, Brigitte, "Die Maßnahmen der Republik Österreich für die Widerstandskämpfer und Opfer des Nationalsozialismus", in Sebastian Meissl, Klaus-Dieter Mulley & Oliver Rathkolb (ed.), *Verdrängte Schuld, verfehlte Sühne. Entnazifizierung in Österreich 1945–1955*, Vienna, 1986.

Gamsjäger, Helmut, *Die Evangelische Kirche in Österreich in den Jahren 1933 bis 1938 unter besonderer Berücksichtigung der Auswirkungen der deutschen Kirchenwirren*, phil. Diss. Vienna, 1967.

Geyde, G.E.R., *Die Bastionen fielen*, Vienna, 1947.

Goebbels, Joseph, *Tagebücher 1924–1945*, ed. Ralf Georg Reuth, Munich/Zurich, 1992.

Gold, Hugo, *Geschichte der Juden in Wien*, Tel-Aviv, 1966.

Goldhagen, Daniel, *Hitler's Willing Executioners*, New York, 1996.

Greiner, Ulrich, "gottelbock. Hitlers Rede in Wien und ein Gedicht von Ernst Jandl", in *Die Zeit*, Nr. 11, March 11, 1988.

Großberg, Mimi, *Gedichte und kleine Prosa*, Vienna, 1972.

Großberg, Mimi, *Geschichte im Gedicht. Das politische Gedicht der Austro-Amerikanischen Exilautoren des Schicksalsjahres 1938*, New York, 1982.

Haider, Edith, "August 1995. Gedichte", in *Mit der Ziehharmonika. Zeitschrift für Literatur des Exils und des Widerstands*, vol. 16, Nr. 3 (1999).

Haiderer, Rudolfine, *Grüß Gott! Heil Hitler! Freundschaft! Erlebnisse eines Wiener Arbeiterkindes 1926–1945*, Krems, 1995.

Hanisch, Ernst, *Der lange Schatten des Staates. Österreichische Gesellschaftsgeschichte im zwanzigsten Jahrhundert*, Vienna, 1994.

Hanisch, Ernst, "Einleitung des Gesellschaftshistorikers", in Walter Weiss & Ernst Hanisch (ed.), *Vermittlungen. Texte und Kontexte österreichischer Literatur im zwanzigsten Jahrhundert*, Salzburg/Vienna, 1990.

Hartl, Erwin, "Was mag sich Friedrich Torberg gedacht haben", epilogue to Friedrich Torberg, *Auch das war Wien. Roman*, ed. David Axmann & Edwin Hartl, Munich/Vienna, 1984.

Hewig, Kristina, *Ernst Jandl. Versuch einer Monographie*, phil. Diss. Vienna, 1981.

Hoffer, Gerda, *Nathan ben Simon und seine Kinder. Eine europäisch-jüdische Familiengeschichte*, Munich, 1996.

Holton, Milne & Kuhner, Herbert (ed. and trans.), *Austrian Poetry Today/ Österreichische Lyrik heute*, New York, 1985.

Huber, Paul, Gregor Ryndziak and Michael Adler, *FK AUSTRIA MEMPHIS Klubgeschichte*, at www.telecom.at/fak/geschichte/mitte.html

Hummer, Hubert, "Region und Widerstand. Am Beispiel des Salzkammergutes. Der österreichische Widerstand gegen den Nationalsozialismus und seine Verankerung im kollektiven Gedächtnis", in Hubert Hummer, Reinhard Kannonier & Brigitte Kepplinger, *Die Pflicht zum Widerstand*, Vienna, 1986.

Jandl, Ernst, *Gesammelte Werke*, Darmstadt/Neuwied, 1985.

Jochum, Manfred, *Die 1. Republik in Dokumenten und Bildern*, Vienna, 1983.

Kain, Franz, *Am Taubenmarkt*, Vienna/Linz/Weitna, 1991.

Kaiser, Konstantin (ed.), *Theodor Kramer 1897–1958. Dichter im Exil. Aufsätze und Dokumente*, in *Zirkular*, special issue 4 (1983).

Kammerstätter, Peter, *Materialiensammlung über den Widerstands- und Partisanenbewegung WILLY-FRED, Freiheitsbewegung im oberen Salzkammergut - Ausseerland 1943–1945. Ein Beitrag zur Erforschung dieser Bewegung*, Linz, 1978.

Keller, Stefan, *Grüningers Fall. Geschichten von Flucht und Hilfe*, 3rd ed., Zurich, 1994.

Keogh, Dermot, *The Jews in Twentieth-Century Ireland. Refugees, Anti-Semitism and the Holocaust*, Cork, 1998.

Kindermann, Heinz (ed.), *Heimkehr ins Reich. Großdeutsche Dichtung aus Ostmark und Sudetenland 1866–1938*, Leipzig, 1938.

Klemperer, Victor, *"LTI". Die unbewältigte Sprache. Aus dem Notizbuch eines Philologen*, Munich, 1969.

Klüger, Ruth, *weiter leben. Eine Jugend*, Munich, 1997.

Klusacek, Christiane, Steiner, Herbert & Stimmer, Kurt (ed.), *Dokumentation zur Österreichischen Zeitgeschichte, 1938–1945*, Vienna/Munich, 1980.

Klusacek, Christiane & Stimmer, Kurt (ed.), *Dokumentation zur Österreichischen Zeitgeschichte, 1928–1938*, Vienna/Munich, 1982.

Körber, Lili, *Eine Österreicherin erlebt den Anschluß. Mit Erläuterungen und einem Nachwort von Viktoria Hertling*, Vienna/Munich, 1988.

131

Koppensteiner, Jürgen, "'juble und jodle!' Fünf Gedichte für eine Österreich-Landeskunde", in *Die Unterrichtspraxis*, vol. 20, Nr. 2 (1987).

Kramer, Theodor, *Wien 1938. Die grünen Kader*, Vienna, 1946.

Kreissler, Felix, *Von der Revolution zur Annexion. Österreich 1918 bis 1938*, Vienna, 1970.

Kummerer, Willy (ed.), *1938–1988. Ein Beitrag der Zentralsparkasse und Kommerzialbank zum Gedenkjahr*, Vienna, 1988.

Lachs, Minna, *Warum schaust du zurück? Erinnerungen 1907-1941*, Vienna/Munich/Zurich, 1986.

Langbein, Hermann, "Darf man vergessen?", in Anton Pelinka & Erika Weinzierl (ed.), *Das große Tabu. Österreichs Umgang mit seiner Vergangenheit*, Vienna, 1987.

Lothar, Ernst, *Das Wunder des Überlebens. Erinnerungen und Ergebnisse*, Vienna/Hamburg, 1961.

Maleta, Alfred, "Bewältigte Vergangenheit", in Kummerer, Willy (ed.), *1938-1988*, Vienna, 1988.

Malina, Peter & Spann, Gustav, *1938 - 1988. Vom Umgang mit unserer Vergangenheit*, Vienna, 1988.

Menasse, Robert, "Im Anfang war das Neue Österreich. Die Erschaffung des österreichischen Überbaus", in R.M., *Überbau und Underground. Die sozialpartnerische Ästhetik. Essays zum österreichischen Geist*, Stuttgart, 1997.

Mann, Klaus, *Der Vulkan. Roman unter Emigranten*, Berlin/Weimar, 1969.

Marx, Karl & Engels, Friedrich, *Das kommunistische Manifest*, Leipzig, 1976.

Mayer-Limberg, Josef, *Fon da Möada und de Hausmasda: Gedichda aus Oddagring*, Graz, 1979.

Mehring, Walter, "Die letzten Stunden", in Ulrich Weinzierl (ed.), *Österreichs Fall. Schriftsteller berichten vom "Anschluß"*, Vienna/Munich, 1988.

Meissl, Sebastian, Mulley, Klaus-Dieter & Rathkolb, Oliver (ed.), *Verdrängte Schuld, verfehlte Sühne. Entnazifizierung in Österreich 1945–1955*, Vienna, 1986.

Mitterer, Felix, *Kein schöner Land. Ein Theaterstück und sein historischer Hintergrund*, Innsbruck, 1987.

Moser, Jonny, "Die Katastrophe der Juden in Österreich 1938-1945 - ihre Voraussetzungen und ihre Überwindung", in *Der gelbe Stern in Österreich. Katalog und Einführung zu einer Dokumentation. Studia Judaica Austriaca*, vol. V, Eisenstadt, 1977.

Müller, Hans-Harald, "*Mainacht in Wien*. Das Bild des 'Anschlusses' in einem Romanfragment von Leo Perutz", in Donald G. Daviau, *Austrian Writers and the Anschluß. Understanding the Past - Overcoming the Past*, Riverside, CA., 1991.

Pabisch, Peter, "Sprachliche Struktur und assoziative Thematik in Ernst Jandls experimentellem Gedicht 'wien: heldenplatz', in *Modern Austrian Literature*, vol. 9, Nr. 2 (1976).

Pelinka, Anton & Weinzierl, Erika (ed.), *Das große Tabu. Österreichs Umgang mit seiner Vergangenheit*, Vienna, 1987.

Perutz, Leo, "Ringsum Stacheldraht. Aus dem Romanfragment 'Mainacht in Wien', geschrieben im Jahr 1938 - II. Teil", in *Die Presse*, April 23/24, 1988.

Prusnik-Gasper, Karel, *Gemsen auf der Lawine. Der Kärtner Partisanenkampf*, Klagenfurt, 1980.

Qualtinger, Helmut, *Der Herr Karl*, in *Qualtingers beste Satiren. Vom Travnicek zum Herrn Karl*, ed. Brigitte Erbacher, Frankfurt a.M., 1976.

Rathgorb, Oliver, Duchkowitsch, Wolfgang & Hausjell, Fritz (ed.), *Die veruntreute Wahrheit. Hitlers Propagandisten in Österreich '38*, Salzburg, 1988.

Rebhahn, Fritz M., *Die braunen Jahre. Wien 1938–1945*, Vienna, 1995.

Rezzori, Gregor von, *Memoiren eines Antisemiten*, excerpted in Ulrich Weinzierl (ed.), *Österreichs Fall. Schriftsteller berichten vom "Anschluß"*, Vienna/Munich, 2nd ed., 1988.

Rosenkranz, Herbert, *Verfolgung und Selbstbehauptung. Die Juden in Österreich 1938-1945*, Vienna/Munich, 1978.

Rotenberg, Stella, *Scherben sind endlicher Hort. Ausgewählte Lyrik und Prosa*, ed. Primus-Heinz Kucher & Armin A. Wallas, Vienna, 1991.

Roth, Joseph, *Werke*, vol. 3: *Das journalistische Werk 1929–1939*, ed. K. Westermann, Cologne, 1991.

Sargardoy, P. Antonio, *Gelegen und Ungelegen. Die Lebenshingabe von Sr. Restituta*, Vienna, 1996.

Scheitauer, Erich et al., *Geschichte Österreichs in Stichworten. Teil VI: Vom Ständestaat zum Staatsvertrag von 1934 bis 1955*, Vienna, 1984.

Schifter, Richard, Foreword to Elfriede Schmidt, *1938... and the Consequences. Questions and Answers*, trans. Peter J. Lyth, Riverside, CA., 1992.

Schmidt, Elfriede, *1938... and the Consequences. Questions and Answers*, transl. Peter J. Lyth, Riverside, CA, 1992.

Schöffling, Klaus & Schütz, Hans J. (ed.), *Almanach der Vergessenen*, Munich, 1985.

Schönberner, Gerhard (ed.), *Wir haben es gesehen. Augenzeugenberichte über Terror und Judenverfolgung im Dritten Reich*, Hamburg, 1962.

Sereny, Gitta, *The German Trauma: Experiences and Reflections 1938–2000*, Harmondsworth, 2000.

Sperber, Manès, *Bis man mir die Scherben auf die Augen legt*, Zurich, 1984.

Sperber, Manès, *Wie eine Träne im Ozean. Romantrilogie. 2. Buch: Tiefer als der Abgrund*, Munich, 1980.

Spiel, Hilde, *Die hellen und die finsteren Zeiten. Erinnerung 1911–1946*, Munich, 1989.

Spira, Leopold, *Feindbild "Jud"'. 100 Jahre Antisemitismus in Österreich*, Vienna/Munich, 1981.

Steiner, Herbert (ed.), *Käthe Leichter: Leben und Werk*, Vienna, 1973.

Steinmayr, Jochen, "Vier Tage, die Österreich berauschten. Ein halbes Jahrhundert später erinnern sich Zeugen an Hitlers Triumphzug nach Wien", in: *Die Zeit*, Nr 11, March 11, 1988.

Stern, Willy, "Viele 'Freunde' wurden Feinde", in: Willy Kummerer (ed.) *1938–1988*, Vienna, 1988.

Stojka, Ceija, *Wir leben im Verborgenen: Erinnerungen einer Rom-Zigeunerin*, ed. Karin Berger, Vienna, 1988.

Szabo, Wilhelm, "Nach dem Entscheid", in Arthur West (ed.), *Linkes Wort für Österreich*, Vienna, 1985.

Thöni, Hans, "Der Anlaß zum Stück: Das Schicksal des Rudolf Gomperz", in Felix Mitterer, *Kein schöner Land. Ein Theaterstück und sein historischer Hintergrund*, Innsbruck, 1987.

Torberg, Friedrich, *Auch das war Wien. Roman*, ed. David Axmann & Edwin Hartl, Munich/Vienna, 1984.

Ungar, Frederick (ed.), *Austria in Poetry and History*, New York, 1984.

Utgaard, Peter, "From *Blümchenkaffee* to *Wiener Melange*: Schools, Identity and Birth of the 'Austria-as-Victim' Myth, 1945–55", in *Austrian History Yearbook*, vol. 30 (1999).

Viertel, Berthold, *Daß ich in dieser Sprache schreibe. Gesammelte Gedichte*, ed. Günther Fetzer, Munich, 1981.

Vogel, Alois, *Schlagschatten - Totale Verdunkelung. Zwei Romane*, ed. August Obermayer & Wendelin Schmidt-Dengler, Vienna/Munich, 1999.

Wagner, Wilhelm J., *Der große Bildatlas zur Geschichte Österreichs*, Vienna, 1995.

Wallas, Armin A., "'Dennoch schreibe ich' – eine Annäherung an das literarische Werk von Stella Rotenberg", in Stella Rotenberg, *Scherben sind endlicher Hort. Lyrik und Prosa*, Vienna, 1991.

Wander, Fred, *Das gute Leben. Erinnerungen*, Munich/Vienna, 1996.

Weinheber, Josef, *Gedichte*, ed. Friedrich Sacher, 2nd ed., Hamburg, 1978.

Weinzierl, Erika, "Der österreichische Widerstand gegen den Nationalsozialismus 1938–1945", in: Erich Zöllner (ed.), *Revolutionäre Bewegungen in Österreich*, Vienna, 1981.

Weinzierl, Ulrich (ed.), *Österreichs Fall. Schriftsteller berichten vom "Anschluß"*, Vienna/Munich, 1988.

Weiss, Walter & Hanisch, Ernst (ed.), *Vermittlungen. Texte und Kontexte österreichischer Literatur im zwanzigsten Jahrhundert*, Salzburg/Vienna 1990.

Welt Trahan, Elizabeth, *Walking with Ghosts. A Jewish Childhood in Wartime Vienna*, New York etc., 1998.

Werfel, Franz, *Cella oder Die Überwinder. Versuch eines Romans*, Frankfurt a.M., 1982.

Wimmer, Adi (ed.), *Strangers at Home and Abroad. Recollections of Austrian Jews Who Escaped Hitler*, Jefferson, N.C./London, 2000.

Wistrich, Robert S. (ed.), *Austrians and Jews in the Twentieth Century. From Franz Joseph to Waldheim*, New York, 1992.

Zuckmayer, Carl, *Als wär's ein Stück von mir. Horen der Freundschaft*, Frankfurt a.M., 1977.

Zweig, Stefan, *Das lyrische Werk (c)*, Frankfurt a.M., 1967.

Zweig, Stefan, *Die Welt von gestern. Erinnerungen eines Europäers*, Vienna, 1948.

Index

German Army, 12
Germany, 2f.
Gestapo, 12, 20, 67, 71, 78, 89, 97f.,
    103, 109
Geyde, G.E.R., 11, 45
Globocnik, Odilo, 88, 101
Gmunden, 73
Goebbels, Josef, 4, 6, 14, 16, 108
Goldhagen, Daniel, 54
Gömbös, Gyula, 1
Gomperz, Rudolf, 109ff.
Göring, Hermann, 4, 6, 13, 36, 77
Graz, 4, 72
Greece, 1
Greiner, Ulrich, 25
Großberg, Mimi, 7, 92f.
Grünbaum, Fritz, 74

Haider, Edith, 116
Haiderer, Rudolfine, 26
Hanisch, Ernst, 24, 29, 40
Hapsburg, Otto von, 3
Hapsburgs, the, 2f.
Hartl, Erwin, 42
Heimwehr, 50, 78
Heydrich, Reinhard, 13, 32
Himmler, Heinrich, 13, 18
Hirsch-Gereuth, Clara von, 92
Hitler Youth, 16f., 29, 48, 51
Hitler, Adolf, 1, 3f., 6, 12ff., 22ff.,
    43ff., 77, 101, 110, 114
Hoare, Samuel, 81
Hofer, Andreas, 5
Hoffer, Gerda, 7, 73
Hull, Cordell, 82, 106
Hungary, 1, 81

Innitzer, Cardinal Theodor, 20, 43f.,
    78
Innsbruck, 5
Ireland, 81
Israelitisches Blindeninstitut, 92f.
Italy, 2f.
Izbica, 117

Jagoda, Leo, 72
Jahn, Friedrich Ludwig,
    "Turnvater", 32
Jandl, Ernst, 23ff., 44
Jansa, Alfred, 4
Joyce, James, 24, 69
Jüdisches Nachrichtenblatt, 63
July Agreement (1936), 3, 15

Kafka, Franz, 79
Kafka, Helena, 75ff., 99
Kain, Franz, 63
Kalmar, Rudolf, 72
Kaltenbrunner, Ernst, 101, 107
Kammerstätter, Peter, 104f.
Kampstein, Lisl, 8
Kauer, Robert, 44
Keller, Paul Anton, 19
Kernstock, Fr. Ottokar, 37
Ketteler, Wilhelm von, 13
Klaar, Ernst, 8
Klaar, Stella, 8
Klagenfurter Zeitung, 37
Kleinmann, Fritz, 57
Klemperer, Viktor, 36, 101
Kloepfer, Hans, 29, 38
Klosterneuburg, 50, 52
Klüger, Ruth, 58, 96
Köhler, Leo, 73
Königswarter, Moritz von, 92
Koppensteiner, Jürgen, 25
Körber, Lili, 2, 5, 11, 14, 41, 78
Kramer, Max, 68
Kramer, Rosa, 88
Kramer, Theodor, 65, 68, 84ff., 99ff.
Kronenzeitung, 55
Kruckenkreuz, 1, 6, 14, 26
Kuffner, Ignaz & Jakob, 20

Lachs, Minna, 22, 27, 30, 49, 97f.
Lackenbach, 102
Langbein, Hermann, 107
Lauterbach, Leo, 49
League of Nations, 15
Legitimists, 3, 6, 98
Leichter, Franzl, 89
Leichter, Heinz, 89
Leichter, Käthe, 89f., 99
Leichter, Otto, 89
Lemberg (Lwów), 109
Lexer, Georg, 42
Liberals, 6
Linz, 5, 16f., 20, 105, 112
Lodz, 88
Loebel, Dr. 14
Loewy, Dr., 41
Lothar, Ernst, 14
Lublin, 88, 101f.
Ludwig, Eduard, 14

Majdanek, 101
Maleta, Alfred, 71